A CANNONEER IN NAVAJO COUNTRY

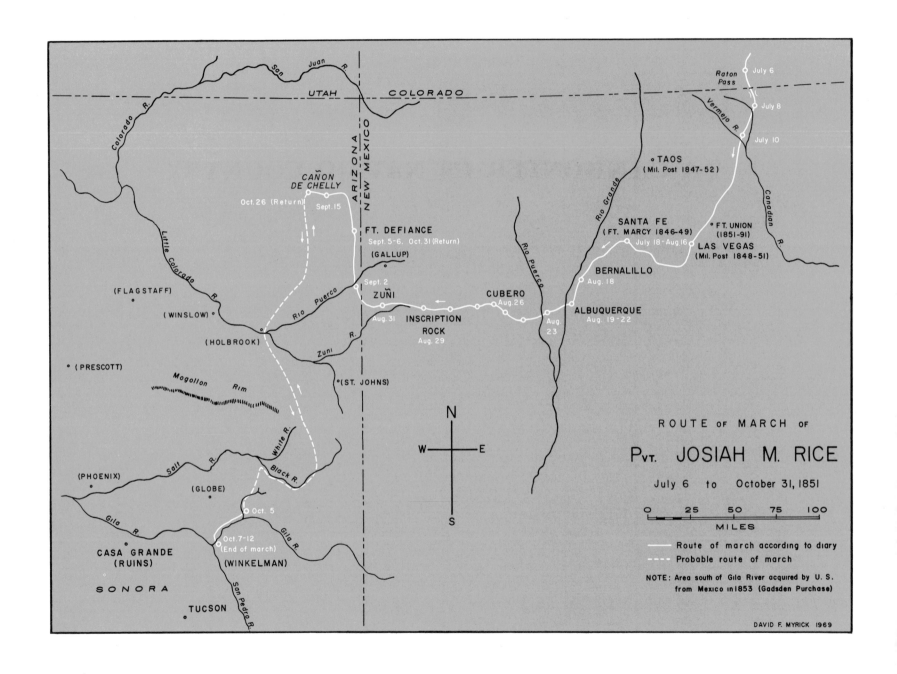

UTAH   COLORADO

San Juan R.

July 6

Raton Pass

July 8

Vermejo R.

July 10

Colorado R.

• TAOS
(Mil. Post 1847-52)

ARIZONA
NEW MEXICO

CAÑON
DE CHELLY

Oct. 26 (Return)   Sept. 15

Little Colorado R.

FT. DEFIANCE
Sept. 5-6. Oct. 31 (Return)

(GALLUP)

Rio Grande

SANTA FE
(FT. MARCY 1846-49)

• FT. UNION
(1851-91)

July 18-Aug. 16

Canadian R.

LAS VEGAS
(Mil. Post 1848-51)

(FLAGSTAFF)
○

Sept. 2

Rio Puerco

ZUÑI

Rio Puerco

BERNALILLO
Aug. 18

CUBERO
Aug. 26

(WINSLOW)
○

Aug. 31

(HOLBROOK)
○

Zuni R.

INSCRIPTION
ROCK
Aug. 29

Aug.
23

ALBUQUERQUE
Aug. 19-22

(PRESCOTT)
○

Mogollon Rim

○(ST. JOHNS)

N

W   ——+——   E

S

ROUTE of MARCH of

P_{VT.} JOSIAH M. RICE

White R.

(PHOENIX)

Salt R.

(GLOBE)

Black R.

Oct. 5

Gila R.

July 6   to   October 31, 1851

0   25   50   75   100
MILES

Oct.7-12
(End of march)

CASA GRANDE
(RUINS)

(WINKELMAN)

—— Route of march according to diary
- - - Probable route of march

SONORA

San Pedro R.

NOTE: Area south of Gila River acquired by U.S.
from Mexico in 1853 (Gadsden Purchase)

TUCSON
○

DAVID F. MYRICK 1969

JOURNAL OF
PRIVATE JOSIAH M. RICE, 1851

A CANNONEER IN NAVAJO COUNTRY

Edited by Richard H. Dillon

PUBLISHED FOR THE DENVER PUBLIC LIBRARY
BY THE OLD WEST PUBLISHING COMPANY·FRED A. ROSENSTOCK
1970

OLD WEST PUBLISHING COMPANY　　•　　1228 EAST COLFAX AVENUE　　•　　DENVER, COLORADO 80218

TABLE OF CONTENTS

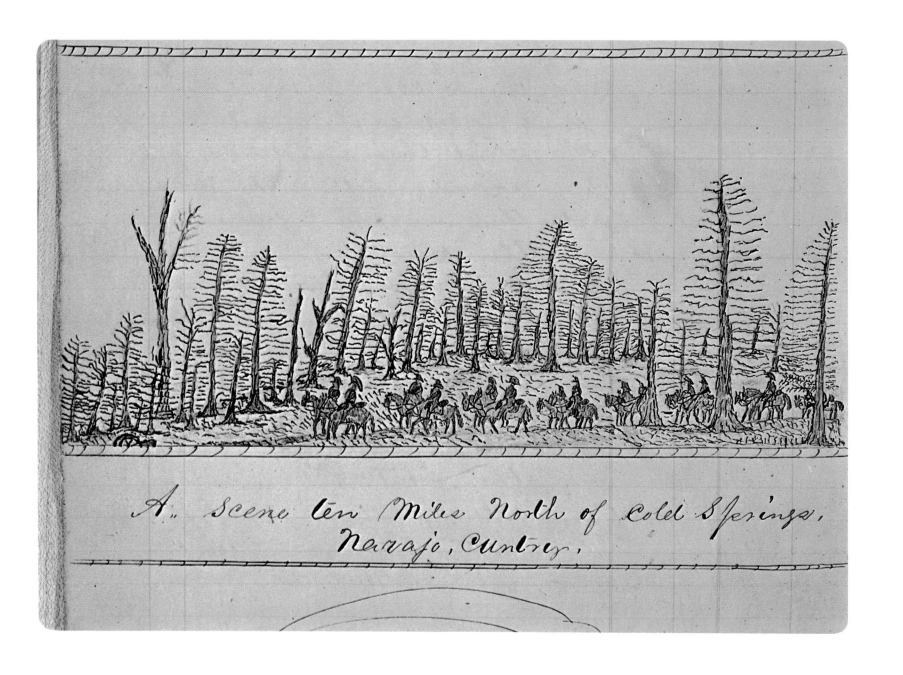

A. Scene ten Miles North of Cold Springs,
Navajo, Cuntrey,

INTRODUCTION

UNEVENNESS IS AS CHARACTERISTIC of the bibliography of Western Americana as it is of the region's terrain. There are enormous ups and downs in the record, ascents and descents which match the mesas and cañons of the West and Southwest. Journals which illuminate the California Gold Rush are almost as common as the proliferating diaries of the Civil War in which, seemingly, every illiterate drummer boy or drunken captain of Volunteers marched to battle with a weapon in one hand and a pen in the other. On the other hand, there was no such comparable urge among the soldiery of the Indian wars to record history as it was being made. Chroniclers were the exception to the rule among officers and virtually unknown in the ranks. Particularly thin are the pickings for the pre-Civil War Indian conflicts and perhaps leanest of all are on-the-spot documents of the Navajo War of the 1850's.

Hence the importance of this narrative by Josiah M. Rice. It is not only the record of a participant in Colonel Edwin Vose Sumner's 1851 sweep through the Navajo country to its very heart, the Cañon de Chelly, it is an artilleryman's account and a private's-eye view of the little-known campaign. Not only does Rice fill us in with details of Sumner's penetration of Cañon de Chelly which are absent from the Colonel's extant reports, he describes the founding of Fort Defiance and its hitherto undocumented first abandonment (reconsidered when supplies finally arrived at the isolated outpost). Most important, perhaps, is Private Rice's account of a virtually unknown reconnaissance in strength of the Gila and San Pedro River country immediately after the Cañon de Chelly expedition of 1851. While Captain Lorenzo Sitgreaves was making his way westward along the Zuñi, Little Colorado and Colorado Rivers that fall of

'51, Lt. Charles A. Griffin of B company, 2d Artillery, was leading a detachment of Sumner's command including Cannoneer Rice in a great sweep from Chinle to the Gila-San Pedro confluence and back to Fort Defiance.

Private Rice, in invading Navajoland, was playing a minor role early in the last act of an almost interminable drama. The curtain had risen on the tragedy some time in 1774, probably, with the first real Spanish confrontation with the *Diné,* "The People," as the Navajos called themselves. It would not lower until 1867 and the reverse-Long March of the Navajos back from Bosque Redondo exile to their tribal homeland of Chuska, Tenucha, and Chelly. During Spanish and Mexican times in New Mexico/Arizona, the Navajo War was an ebb and flow of raids and skirmishes, a continual guerrilla warfare broken only by brief relapses into uneasy truces which masqueraded as peace. Matters were no different during the early *Yanqui* period in the Southwest. Although the bloody Apache conflict of later years placed it in the shade, the Navajo War was no paper affair. According to the bible of military historians, Francis B. Heitman's *Historical Register and Dictionary of the American Army,* 2,561 troops were engaged, of whom 1,500 were Regulars and the remainder militiamen.

Private Josiah M. Rice was, just possibly, the West's worst speller although Meriwether Lewis' crony, William Clark, might give him a tussle at originality of orthography. The Editor has cleaned up the young artilleryman's spelling in order to make the narrative readable–for it is a fascinating story once the underbrush of misspelling and pidgin-Spanish is cleared out–but has taken *no* liberties with the cannoneer's ideas and virtually none in his phrasing and grammar. Scholars who wish to study every barbarism of the partially-educated private are urged to see the original journal. It is in the Western History Department of the Denver Public Library. For those of more casual curiosity, the Editor has left Rice's Fort Defiance poem, "Valley of the Diamonds," which follows the table of distances closing the narrative, in its original state of orthographic sin.

Against this sole weakness of misspelling, Rice mustered a whole platoon of assets. He was young, energetic, and curious as a cat. He saw things from the lowly viewpoint of the private soldier and raw recruit, not the educated career officer. Thus, he was able to suggest the macabre humor of the enlisted men, as when some of the rank and file, for a lark, made a mummified Indian "walk" about Chouteau's Island on improvised stilts. He conveyed the nervousness of the combat soldier, inflating in his mind the strength of the enemy while his stomach and heart, both, shriveled inside him in apprehension. Finally, Cannoneer Rice suffered not only from a compulsion to write down everything of importance which he viewed while campaigning but also was persuaded to enhance his journal with splendid, if naive, drawings of what he saw along his route of march. Rice's pictures, like those of Sam Chamberlain or Father Nicholas Point, have a freshness because of their naivete and immediacy which suggest the artist's role as *participant* in the drama of the Southwestern frontier far more than the polished, redrawn, and lithographed or engraved views of the Railroad Surveys or John R. Bartlett's *Narrative of Explorations.* We can be grateful, indeed, that young Rice decided to "improve the leisure opportunities by keeping a small journal," and, particularly, by deciding to illustrate it.

Despite his god-awful spelling, Rice's journal is blessed, from time to time, with examples of quite graceful writing. For example, on the long march westward from Fort Leavenworth toward the mountains, he wrote: "Perhaps it is one of the most beautiful sights in nature to see a puff of wind sweep over these grassy plains, turning the glistening sides of the grass to the sun and seeming to spread a stream of light along the surface of the wave, like a surge at sea." No doubt about it, the 19-year old artilleryman had a streak of poetry in his nature.

Rice gave his age as 27 years when he enlisted, on November 16, 1861. But according to his 1914 death certificate he was born on December 7, 1832. His birthplace, again according to his Lansing, Michigan, death certificate, was "Lisbeth," New York. This was Elizabethtown in upstate New York's Clinton County in the Adirondacks. The friends to whom he bade farewell as he left for his New Mexico adventure were largely in Elizabethtown and Plattsburgh, in neighboring Essex County, New York. When he returned from the Navajo War to civilian life, it was to a career as a carpenter in Schuyler Falls, Clinton County, and it was there that he reenlisted for Civil War service. His experiences in the War of the Rebellion are documented in another journal held by the Denver Public Library's Western History Department.

From the tone of a single surviving letter, printed in this volume after the Navajo War narrative, Rice's mother was a devout woman. She was apparently a remarried widow since Rice addressed a letter to her as (Mrs.) P. H. Graves. Curiously, Rice's death certificate bears the name of his father, Loran {sic} Rice but the doctor wrote "not known" in the space on the form for the deceased's mother's name. The young soldier's uncle, G. W. Brown, was the well-known publisher of the Conneautville *Courier,* in Pennsylvania's "Far West"–Crawford County, near Erie. Rice, although no speller, was middling-well educated for his age and obviously a reader, for his journal entries refer to the works of William Cullen Bryant, James Fenimore Cooper, and other writers. This little conceit is common enough in 19th century American diaries and journals, to be sure, but considerably less so in those of teen-aged artillerymen on the Navajo frontier.

The backdrop to Rice's adventures in the Southwest was a federal Indian policy dominated by a seesawing between pleas and threats. Initially peaceful overtures by the military were uniformly followed by shows of strength as the Navajos failed to live up to half-understood treaty vows and pledges made by a handful of chiefs. This alternation between carrot and club, bribe and bullying, was a policy of expediency which was fore-doomed to failure. Two of the most obvious reasons for this fate were the relative feebleness of the forces committed to the vast area of the Southwest after the close of the Mexican War, and the fact that the military presence was superimposed upon the enmity of decades between Navajos and settled folk. The Navajos found the Pueblos and the New Mexicans to be their natural enemies in an almost ecological sense. Raiding was a way of life with the Navajos and they were not about to give it up in the face of warnings from a handful of soldiers hard put to garrison and defend long-established Rio Grande Valley settlements, much less pacify the countryside or invade the wilderness of Arizona on punitive raids against the *Diné*. At the time Artilleryman Rice was soldiering in the Southwest, New Mexico Indian Agent John Greiner estimated that he and his fellow troopers were outnumbered by almost one hundred-to-one odds.

Relations between the United States and the Navajo nation were less cordial, at first, than the initial contacts between Yankees and Apaches but far less bellicose than those with the Sioux or Blackfeet. But what friendship existed soon evaporated before the burning hatred of the *Diné* for the Pueblos and *Nuevo Mexicanos* whom the Americans, victorious in the Mexican War, were sworn to protect. The enmity was quickly returned by both military and civil authorities in the new Territory and, eventually, General James H. Carleton, of California Column fame, and Colonel Kit Carson had to literally uproot the Navajos and transport them to a detention camp at Bosque Redondo where they could be closely watched from Fort Sumner.

But the Long Walk of 1863 to Bosque Redondo was preceded by a series of largely indecisive punitive campaigns mounted by the Army against the Navajos, one of which was Colonel Edwin V. Sumner's 1851 expedition, on which Private Josiah Rice marched. The first Army action of all took place on September 16, 1846 when General Stephen W. Kearny ordered Colonel Alexander W. Doniphan to station three companies of his regiment of Missouri Mounted Volunteers, under Lt. Colonel Charles F. Ruff, at the town of Cebolleta. From this oniony settlement sixty miles west of Albuquerque, the horse soldiers were to interdict Navajo raids against New Mexico's settlements. However, the soldiers were so few and their nags so worn by the long march from Fort Leavenworth that they posed little of an obstacle to *Diné* raiders. Horse soldiers proved to be no better than infantrymen or dismounted dragoons at catching Navajos. Indian Agent Greiner knew why; a mounted dragoon would weigh 225 pounds with all of his gear. On a horse good only for carrion, he could never close with an Indian toting only a bow and arrow on a fresh pony. And, to boot, the trooper knew nothing of the country which was home to the Navajo warrior.

Because depredations continued, Kearny called on Doniphan in October of 1846 to mount a punitive expedition. Major William Gilpin marched from Abiquiu, where he had been keeping an eye peeled for Utes, and Lt. Colonel Cosgreve Jackson from Cebolleta to a rendezvous with Doniphan at Ojo del Oso, or Bear Springs, fifteen miles east of today's Gallup, on the slopes of the Zuñi Mountains above the Rio Puerco Valley. The Army made use of the services of Antonio Sandoval, alias Crooked Foot, chief of the so-called Enemy Navajos. The latter had split away from the *Diné* and allied themselves with New Mexicans and *gringos* against their kin. In fact, Sandoval was not above enslaving his own people and selling them to the New Mexicans. Old Chief Narbona and several thousand Navajos finally came to talk peace. He and Zarcillas Largas (Long Earrings) agreed to a peace with the Puebloans and New Mexicans, promising to return slaves and captured animals to the settlements.

The treaty meant almost nothing to the Navajos. They continued to plunder exposed settlements of their herds and to seize captives with impunity. The Army was finally convinced that Doniphan's treaty was abrogated and Major W. H. T. Walker, on September 10, 1847, led a battalion of Missouri Volunteers (every man jack drunk as a lord) to Ojo del Oso, Laguna Colorada (Red Lake), and into awesome Cañon de Chelly itself. Walker penetrated the gorge from the east for about six miles until his nerves persuaded him to turn back from a potential ambush. He retreated to Santa Fe but his mere presence in the heartland of the *Diné* did some good. A delegation of headmen followed him to the capital to arrange a council in which they agreed to leave the settlements in peace.

Walker's *pax* was shortlived, lasting only through the blasts of winter and until spring planting. By March, with their corn crop secure, the Navajos were ready for their seasonal raids. The new C.O. of the 9th Military Department, Colonel E. W. Newby, bolstered his thin line of men by mustering militia units from among the New Mexican settlers. On May 1, 1848, he took the field and engaged in a few brushes with the enemy. His column was not powerful enough to hurt the Navajos badly but it persuaded them to sign yet another treaty. To the *Diné*, the "New Men," *Anglos,* seemed even more bewitched by the inking of paper than the Spaniards and Mexicans of yore.

On July 22, 1849, James S. Calhoun arrived in Santa Fe to take office as Indian Agent for New Mexico. He sized up the shaky truce as merely a device of the Navajos which allowed them to raid or not raid, as they pleased. He also feared that they were beginning to consider the Americans to be too weak to punish them. To educate them to the incorrectness of this idea, Calhoun worked with the new military governor of New Mexico, Brevet Lieutenant Colonel John M. Washington, who arrived in Fort Marcy (Santa Fe) on October 10, 1848. Together they planned an expedition to put the fear of God–and Uncle Sam–into the *Diné*. On April 16, 1849, Washington's first units marched out of the capital, bound for a rendezvous at Jemez Pueblo. There the Volunteer Company garrisoning Jemez joined them.

Guided by the ubiquitous Antonio Sandoval of the Enemy Navajo, Washington started his command for the legendary redoubt of the Navajos, Cañon de Chelly. After a difficult passage through Chaco Cañon, the small army reached the Tunicha Valley where a pow-wow was bungled by them.

Lieutenant James Simpson then reconnoitered the great chasm with sixty men, searching for the "Navajo fort" supposed to lie in its depths. He did not find the fortress, of which the Spaniards and Mexicans had spoken for so long, because it did not exist. Perhaps the legend referred to the White House ruin or, more likely, to Massacre Cave in the tributary Cañon del Muerto. Actually, Cañon de Chelly itself was the Navajos' bastion. Simpson and Washington explored the great gash from the west, penetrating it enough to remove the cloud of mystery which had hung over it for years. Simpson's reconnaissance of the terrain was invaluable to later-comers like Col. E. V. Sumner. Simpson advised: "Should it ever be necessary to send troops up the cañon, no obstruction will be found to prevent the passage of artillery along its bottom. And should it, at the same time, which is not at all unlikely, be necessary that a force should skirt the heights above to drive off assailants from that quarter, the south bank should be preferred because {it is} less interrupted by lateral branch cañons." On September 9, 1849, some Navajo chiefs met with Washington and Calhoun to sign a treaty in order to remove the military from their homeland. From Chinle Wash, Colonel Washington made his way back to the Rio Grande via Cañon Bonito and Zuñi.

Washington's treaty was no more viable than its predecessors. Hardly had he turned his back when the Navajos were raiding stock at Zuñi, San Ildefonso, Santo Domingo, Santa Ana, Cebolleta, Abiquiu, Cubero, La Pugarita and Corrales. The retaliation of the New Mexicans and the actions of the slavers, both Indian and Mexican, made matters worse and the strife was compounded when Mexican traders spread the word in order to improve flagging sales of arms to hostiles that the *Anglos*, the Mexicans and the Pueblos were in league to exterminate the *Diné*.

Indian Agent James S. Calhoun got the new military governor, John Munroe, to license traders and forbid all commercial intercourse with Navajos, Utes and Apaches because they were at war, undeclared, to be sure, with the United States. When Zuñi was threatened with virtual siege by the Navajos he gave the pueblo's home guard fifty muskets and sent a dragoon detachment there to beef up the defense.

James S. Calhoun became Governor of New Mexico on March 4, 1851, as well as Superintendent of Indian Affairs. He immediately issued a proclamation to the governors and *caciques* of all pueblos forbidding trade with the Navajos and authorizing these officials to make war on them and to seize and divide up any captured property. The federal government backed Calhoun by replacing Munroe with one of the most prominent officers in the Army, Colonel Edwin Vose Sumner. Not a West Pointer, Sumner had entered the service on March 3, 1818, as an infantry shavetail. After serving in the Black Hawk War he transferred to the Second Dragoons and served under General Winfield Scott in the Mexican War. In New Mexico, he was commander of the Army's Ninth Military Department from 1851 until 1853. He would, eventually, serve as a short-term Governor of New Mexico when illness would force Calhoun to leave office on May 6, 1852. Sumner served in this capacity until relieved by Calhoun's successor, William Carr Lane, who was sworn in on September 13, 1852.

Colonel Sumner's sweeping orders involved the reorganization of the entire defense system in New Mexico. The War Department particularly wanted to move troops out of the Rio Grande Valley towns and to station them on the frontier nearer the hostiles. This suited Sumner perfectly and he wrote his superiors from Fort Union on October 24, 1851: "My first step was to break up the post at Santa Fe, that sink of vice and extravagance, and to remove the troops from the towns of Las Vegas, Rayado, Albuquerque, Cebolleta, Socorro, Doña Ana, San Elizario and El Paso . . . I consider the withdrawal of the troops from the towns a matter of vital importance, both as it regards discipline and economy . . . Most of the troops in this Territory have become, in a high degree, demoralized." Sumner established a chain of military posts–Fort Fillmore on the Rio Grande near El Paso, Fort Conrad near Valverde, Fort Union on the Mora River near Las Vegas and the Santa Fe Trail, and Fort Defiance. This last, the exposed frontier fort in Cañon Bonito became the home of diarist Private Josiah M. Rice for several months.

The key portion of Sumner's instruction brought Private Rice to Navajoland: "From all the information that has reached the Department, it is induced to believe that no permanent peace can exist with the Indians and no treaty will be regarded by them until they have been made to feel the power of our arms. You will, therefore, as early as practicable, make an expedition against the Navajos and also one against the Utahs and Apaches, and inflict upon them a severe chastisement." Unlike Colonel Washington, Sumner wanted no Indian agent along and he did not allow Calhoun to join him, fearing the latter might meddle in Army affairs. As a result, the two became fast enemies.

Sumner was called "Old Martinet" and "The Big Bug of Albuquerque" but he was not stupid or bungling and his 1851 expedition was no less successful, if no more, than those of both his predecessors and successors prior to Colonel Kit Carson. It proved to be the great adventure in the life of Josiah M. Rice. He said goodbye to friends in Elizabethtown and Plattsburgh, New York, and made his way to New York City with the intention to either sign on a whaleship or sail before the mast in a merchantman. Like so many other would-be sailors, when he found no berth, he easily made the switch to the Army. On March 10, 1851, he enlisted for a five-year hitch, giving his age as 22 when he was a little over 18. He did not secure his parent's permission. On October 19, 1852, when he wanted "out," his uncle wrote him, "You were a minor when you enlisted. And if your father was disposed to interest himself in your favor, he could forward your relief." His father was so disposed, apparently, for Rice got his discharge long before his five years were up.

Private Rice was sent from the Recruiting Depot on Bedloe's Island, where the Statue of Liberty would later be erected, to Fort Columbus on Governor's Island just off the Battery. This harbor defense post had been begun in 1806 when Fort Jay (1794-1806) was demolished. Rice was assigned there to the 2nd Regiment of Artillery, a light artillery and howitzer outfit, and he sailed for New Orleans on the *Juliet* shortly, although he was both ill and as grassy-green as any soldier who ever enlisted. The vessel which took him westward was probably the full rigged 524-ton *Juliet*, built at Bath, Maine, in 1848 by William Rogers.

The first leg of the Artilleryman's voyage was uneventful, if a hungry one. He amused himself by staring at passing vessels and observing such landfalls as Grand Abaco in the Bahamas. He also watched the "sea pigs," dolphins or porpoises, as they played alongside the hull. Confusingly, Rice compared the "dolphin" to the trout of Saranac Lake in Franklin County, New York. He was referring, of course, to the fish, Hawaii's *mahi-mahi*, called by the same name as the sea mammal–or else Sara-

nac Lake was a Loch Ness in disguise, as far as its trout were concerned.

The penultimate day of April 1851 saw the *Juliet* swinging at anchor in the muddy outfall of the Mississippi River below New Orleans. The dullness of shipboard life was finally broken when seven of Rice's comrades in arms decided to take French leave. They went over the side, swam ashore and disappeared beyond the levees. Under guard, Rice and the remaining soldiers, who resembled "starving hogs" to the ships' captains who saw them, were herded aboard a steam packet, the *James H. Hewitt*, for the six-day, 1,210-mile passage of the Mississippi River to Jefferson Barracks, Missouri. This post had been set up as Camp Adams in 1826 on the west bank below St. Louis and was still in 1851 the major outfitting point for westward expeditions. The trip to Jefferson Barracks was made without serious incident, except that a thunderstorm blew the *Hewitt's* pilot house overboard.

Safe at Jefferson Barracks, the raw recruits speedily got drunk on rawer whiskey. Less a few more deserters, they bade farewell to Captain Braxton Bragg's garrison and Brevet Major Israel B. Richardson ordered them aboard the chartered steam packet *Arkansas*, bound up-Missouri to Fort Leavenworth. This post, established in 1827 on the west bank of the Big Muddy near the modern city of Leavenworth, Kansas, was the major jumping-off place for expeditions into the Indian country. In a sense, Rice's journey up the Missouri on the *Arkansas* was more harrowing than the desert marches and Navajo skirmishes he would endure in the Southwest, for many of his companions died of cholera on the steamboat. The illness of so many men, when combined with the tardy arrival of two howitzers and eight brass six-pounders from the Springfield Arsenal detained Rice's detachment in Fort Leavenworth until the end of May. So ill was Rice's Company Commander, Captain Henry Lane Kendrick, a favorite of Rice and his battery mates, that he had to be left behind while Second Lieutenant John Creed Moore led the battery out of the Fort on May 30, 1851, bound for Bent's Fort. They were five days behind Colonel Sumner, their commander.

Kendrick, who was a friend of Rice's family, was anything but the typical Army officer of the frontier. He was an intellectual who had been appointed to the Military Academy from New Hampshire, his home-state. Entering West Point on September 1, 1831, he graduated on July 1, 1835, and, as was the custom, was made a brevet second lieutenant that same day. However, he was not sent to garrison with his classmates but, while technically assigned to the 2d Infantry, was posted to West Point itself. There he served from 1835 until 1847 as Assistant Professor and Principal Assistant Professor of Mineralogy and Chemistry. In 1836 he was promoted to second lieutenant and transferred to the 2d Artillery. The following year he was raised to first lieutenant. Made a captain of the 2d Artillery on June 18, 1846, he served with distinction in the Mexican War, especially at the siege of Vera Cruz, the battles of Cerro Gordo, the skirmish at Amazoque, and the defense of Puebla. He was brevetted a major on October 12, 1847, for his gallant and meritorious conduct at Puebla. After garrison duty in New York harbor and at Jefferson Barracks in 1848 and 1849, he was given frontier duty. He led an artillery battalion from Fort Leavenworth to Santa Fe in 1849, then explored New Mexico and fought Navajos until Rice met him in 1851.

Lieutenant Moore was no scholar like Kendrick and his early career was not as brilliant. But the young Tennessean, who became a Confederate brigadier general in the Civil War, was a West Point graduate of 1849 who had ranked seventeenth in his class in academic standing. After serving in Florida during the last of the Seminole troubles, he was assigned to Santa Fe and frontier duty in the late spring of 1851, when Rice met him. He led Rice and his companions safely along the Military Road, or California-Oregon Trail, to its junction with the Santa Fe Trail which they reached on June 4, 1851.

Rice was disappointed by his first view of the Great Plains. He had expected too much. The one thing which he really came to appreciate was the breeze which blew across the dried-up short grass of the Plains with each sundown. And, despite the heat and dust and fatigue, he found his health returning on the march before he even reached Cottonwood Forks of the Neosho River, where Kendrick rejoined his command. Kendrick had been lucky; Colonel Sumner lost his Surgeon, Dr. Alfred W. Kennedy, and some thirty-five men between Fort Leavenworth and the Arkansas before he wore out the cholera on the Plains. The Captain reassumed the command and led his men to Pawnee Forks on June 15, 1851, where Rice tasted his first buffalo meat and was again disappointed. He found it inferior to beef. But the animal itself, live and in the hide, really impressed him. He described the first bison he saw: "The little, glittering, eye shines through an immense mass of long hair which covers the head and neck, giving the creature an exceedingly vicious appearance while the contrast which is afforded between its hind and fore quarters adds materially to its hideousness, for he appears to be all head and shoulders, tapering off at the very point of the tail."

After seeing only a handful of redmen on the march, Rice was overwhelmed by the presence of so many Indians around Bent's Fort. He estimated their number to be 10,000! As an artilleryman, he was pleased to learn of their dread of cannon, which they called "thunder and lightning instruments." Colonel Sumner's rendezvous for the various units of his expedition, strung across the Plains, lay some twelve miles below the Fort. On June 29, 1851, Rice enjoyed (hardly the word!) his first Indian scare there. Major Philip Thompson, a dragoon officer who, somehow, managed to stay drunk every foot of the way from Fort Leavenworth to Bent's Fort, whipped an Indian he found skulking around his tent. (The Georgian was a pretty fair soldier for a drunkard. A West Point

graduate of 1835, he had pulled all kinds of frontier duty between that date and 1851 and was a brevet major as a result of his gallantry at the Battle of Sacramento near Chihuahua in 1847. He would serve on Indian scouts long after Rice first met him but was finally cashiered in 1855 for disrespect to a courtmartial when he appeared as a very intoxicated witness in a case. He became William Walker's adjutant general in the filibustering expedition of 1856-1858 to Nicaragua but died in the Gulf of Mexico in 1857.) The Indians did not react to Thompson's drubbing of one of their number but their anger simmered.

A second incident nearly brought Rice into his first combat action. An Army horse strayed into the Indian camp. Not only did the redskins fail to return it, they refused to do so and chased away a corporal's guard sent to retrieve the mount. Colonel Sumner said little or nothing in public but led forty dragoons, personally, into camp to seize the horse. Besides the matter of military "face," mounts were valuable and in very short supply. So many of the artillery horses had been killed off by the grueling march across the High Plains that Sumner had to replace them at Bent's Fort with draught mules. Rice later estimated that of the 100 fine cannon horses which had started out, not more than ten reached Santa Fe.

Sumner had hardly started his command on the road to Santa Fe again when a hard-riding express galloped up to tell him that the Indians were trying to take Bent's Fort. It turned out to be pure bluff; when Sumner showed fight, the redskins not only backed down but, according to Private Rice, fled across the plain like antelope. Sumner was able to leave Bent's Fort, for the second time, on July 9, 1851. According to David Lavender, historian of Bent's Fort, the confrontation between the Cheyenne loafers and Bull-Head Sumner, so called because a musket ball had once bounced off his skull, was caused not by Thompson's lambasting the snooper nor Sumner's retrieval of the strayed Army horse but by the Colonel's carelessness in allowing green recruits, like Rice, to fraternize freely with the Indians. Tom (Broken Hand) Fitzpatrick did not like it and said, later, "Such free and unrestrained intercourse carried on between officers, privates, squaws and Indians . . . was certainly a new thing to me." Sumner ignored the feelings and, probably, warnings of men like Fitzpatrick until the incident which the mountain men anticipated finally occurred. A Cheyenne chief forcibly took a ring off the finger of an Army officer's wife. Naturally, she screamed for her husband and he lashed the Indian across the face with a buggy whip. Such an act was as great an insult to an Indian as was the liberty the chief had taken to a white man. The medicine man, Bear, began to preach war to the tribe. Fitzpatrick and Bent cooled off the chiefs, however, and with Sumner's show of force, the Indians, prudently, decided to let the gross insult pass.

Colonel Sumner had his own version of the affair, which he stated to Adjutant General Jones in a letter of October 24, 1851: "On my arrival at the post on the Arkansas, I found a large number of Indians collected there of various tribes. Some uneasiness appeared among the Cheyennes and as I was marching past their village, several shots were fired towards the rear of my column. At the same time, I received a note from the Indian Agent, to look out for them, as they were bent on mischief. I immediately countermarched a company of horse and remained near the village till my train had passed. No further hostility was then shown by the Indians. On the following night I received a letter from Brevet Lieutenant Colonel {William} Hoffman, the Commander of the new post, informing me that the Indians were evidently banding together and it was thought they intended some act of hostility. At the dawn of the day, the next morning, I marched back with my whole command. I assembled a number of the chiefs and head men and said to them I had come back to meet them as friends or enemies, it was for them to say which, but they must say it immediately. They at once disclaimed all intention of hostility and I resumed my march."

The first New Mexican settlement which Rice saw was Mora, on July 13. A few adobe huts which had just survived a Navajo raid, Mora did not impress the New Yorker. He was disillusioned already by the Spanish Southwest, writing "Nothing could be more discouraging to men fated to remain a whole year in New Mexico Territory than the first view of the town." Mora had been settled in 1835 as Ojo de Santa Gertrudis de Mora—St. Gertrude's Spring, of the Mulberry River. When some

French trappers camped there and found human bones in the water, they naturally changed the name to the grisly *L'eau des Morts* (River of the Dead). Comanches raided the settlement first, then Texans in 1843 and, finally, Navajos in 1851.

Sumner's soldiers were worried over possible Navajo attacks in the mountain passes but they reached Las Vegas without suffering an ambush. The first settlement here on the Gallinas River in the 1820's had failed because of Indian hostility but in 1833 a group of men from San Miguel del Vado secured a grant and began a permanent town. By 1846, it had grown into a town which Dr. Adolphus Wislizenus could describe as "100 bad houses and poor, dirty looking, inhabitants." General Stephen Watts Kearny in 1847 made it U.S. Army headquarters and it so remained until Fort Union was established in the year of Rice's arrival in New Mexico. At Las Vegas a Navajo was taken prisoner but he turned out to be a son of the old collaborator chief of the Enemy Navajos, Sandoval. He told Sumner that only á tribal quarrel had prevented Chief Carvajal from attacking the command in the Pecos Mountains. The identity of this Carvajal is not known. He was not, of course, the Mexican from San Isidro whom Lt. James H. Simpson in 1849 found "a most excellent guide" in his march to Cañon de Chelly. Nor does it seem likely he was the Carvajal, or Savayaan, of the Tabaha Clan of the Enemy Navajo, unless he was the *Diné* equivalent of an 1851 double-agent.

Rice reached San Miguel del Vado at the Pecos River ford and there saw his first *acequia* or irrigation ditch, which he called a "zaky." From there, his route of march led him to the ruins of storied Pecos where he learned of the legend of Montezuma's undying fire and the race of white giants who had once dwelt there. Rice even saw bones which, he claimed, were those of a man at least ten feet tall. Arrived in Santa Fe, the young Cannoneer examined and described the capital in detail. It was the Army's 9th Military Department headquarters, commanded by Colonel John Munroe. The latter was Military Governor of New Mexico, until the day of Rice's arrival, July 19, 1851, when Colonel Edwin Vose Sumner relieved him. Rice noticed that Colonel Brooks had his artillery pieces ranged across the Plaza opposite the Palace of the Governors, that citizens of Santa Fe were addicted to garlic and *cigaritos,* and that funerals (especially of children) were frequent in the city of the Holy Faith. Moreover, he noted that poor, or lazy, parents in mourning often stole crosses from old graves in order to erect them over the remains of their newly-departed loved ones.

On August 17, 1851, Major Kendrick led Rice and his comrades out of Santa Fe, heading for Navajo country. The dates and distances given by Dragoon James A. Bennett for the Sumner expedition, published as *Forts and Forays* by University of New Mexico Press in 1948 do not correspond with Rice's. Some of the difference is due to the fact that Sumner broke his command into several segments to insure enough water and forage at his camps; more of it is due to the fact that Bennett garbled his dates badly. A better "control" is the 1851 journal of Richard Kern* whose dates do not always agree with Rice's but the former marched with Captain Lorenzo Sitgreaves' unit where the artilleryman was with Sumner's main body of troops. Sumner had four dragoon companies, and Rice's Company B, 2d Artillery, with its two field howitzers (one a six-pounder and one a twelve-pounder), two twelve-pound mountain howitzers, and two caissons. From the capital they marched to Galisteo Creek, where Sumner encamped downstream from Santo Domingo. Rice found the settlement to be a beautiful one—"It has a very pretty appearance, every house surrounded by fruit trees." Alas, the flood of 1886 washed away the handsome settlement of two-story adobe houses with windows glazed with gypsum. The present Santo Domingo was built at that time. Sitgreaves' detachment was already camped at Santo Domingo by the 13th, according to Kern, and it left the next day and camped five miles south, where Sumner joined it on the 15th.

Down the Rio Grande marched the column. According to Richard Kern's notes, the march proceeded thus—on August 17th to Angosturas, to Bernalillo on the 18th. On the 19th Sumner passed Sitgreaves and camped below Sandia. On the 29th, Sitgreaves, Kern *et al* camped oppo-

site Albuquerque, near Sumner. Rice reported the Alcalde of Albuquerque to be no one but the ex-Governor of New Mexico, Manuel Armijo. From Albuquerque, the troopers began a parching march westward, reaching and following the dry bed of the cottonwood-fringed Puerco River on the 22d, passing the scant water of Sheep Springs at about 4 p.m. that day, seeing Casa Colorada, and reaching the pueblo of Laguna. Rice was much taken with this settlement, too. He compared it in attractiveness with another favorite, Bernalillo, above Albuquerque. According to Kern, Sitgreaves' party passed Rice's artillery unit some miles east of Laguna on Saturday, August 23d. On the 25th, while Rice was at Ojo del Gallo, according to his diary (or Sheep Springs, according to his dated itinerary) Kern was at the "sky pueblo" of Ácoma. The latter camped with Sitgreaves next day on the edge of the *pedregal*, the lava malpais south of modern Grants, New Mexico. He did not reach Ojo del Gallo or "Rooster Springs" until the rainy 27th of August. Then, according to Kern, Sumner and presumably Rice were not there but encamped some miles to the south and east, without grass or water.

Cubero, that old last outpost for raids and counter-raids on the Navajo frontier, was a fair sight to Rice's tired eyes. He was sick as well as fatigued, bouncing along in a wagon bed when the prettiest girl in all of New Mexico (he insisted) took pity on him there, smiled and said, *"Pobrecito!"* These words to the lonely young private in his fever were "the sweetest of all sweet

---

* "Part of Col. Sumner's Navajo Chastising Expedition Camped at Santo Domingo." Huntington Library Manuscript HM 4277, volumes I and II.

sounds." Rice and his comrades, sick or well, could not tarry in Cubero. Just prior to their arrival, the Navajos had run off the town's stock so the troopers plunged eagerly into the wilderness of mesas and cañons in hopes of becoming revenging heroes in the eyes of such fair ones as Rice's sweet-talker. But soon the inevitable rumors began to fly. One of the best was that the enemy not only had rifles and pistols but even cannon captured from troops in Mexico! No wonder that nervous sentries sometimes fired their muskets at shadowy yuccas lurking near camp, in the belief that they were Navajo spies. Ojo del Gallo was a delight to Rice, too, an oasis in the desert, abounding with game from mountain sheep and antelope to "horney frogs" which seemed to carpet the sandy soil with their warty bodies. Next, Rice reached Hay Camp or Owensby Camp, about thirty miles from Laguna and between that pueblo and modern Grants. (There, Americans cutting hay for the Quartermaster in Cubero had been surprised and massacred by Navajos.) According to Kern, he and Sitgreaves rejoined Sumner's command at sunset on the 28th at Willow Springs on the east side of the Zuñi Mountains but near the summit, having taken the new Bishop's Road, El Camino del Obispo, ten miles south of Gallina Springs. This road was built for the passage of their Catholic bishop in 1850 by the Indians of the Laguna, Ácoma, and Zuñi pueblos. From a camp at what Rice called Cold Springs (perhaps at or near Ice Caves??) the artillery made its way to El Morro, or Inscription Rock, which Kern and the Topographical

Engineer, Sitgreaves, reached on the 30th after visiting the rounded megaliths called Los Gigantes. At Ojo del Pescado or Fish Springs, called Boiling Springs, too, the men stripped and waded into the water. They, quite literally, shoveled out enough fish to supply a company mess with breakfast for all hands, next morning. By now, even the torrential rainstorms did not faze the toughening recruits. They were already, in Rice's words, "case-hardened against storms and hardships." Rice failed to mention an annoying incident at Ojo del Pescado which Kern recorded. At the time when, according to Dragoon James Bennett's erroneously-dated account, *Forts and Forays*, the command was supposedly entering Cañon de Chelly, the Navajos were running off the *mulada*. Kendrick or Sitgreaves appealed to Sumner for help after this 10 p.m. raid and, next morning, "Old Bull" sent a dragoon detachment off in pursuit of the rustlers. Forty-five of the stolen mules were found grazing in a cañon and restored to the command.

Richard Kern, Sitgreaves' draughtsman, reported all units camped on the 31st at some tanks or springs six miles east of Zuñi pueblo, with the infantry and Kern's party in good shape but "the dragoons and artillery, as usual, without grass." On the first of September, Sumner held a pow-wow with the Zuñis which Kern reported most succinctly–"Old Bull in council with the Zunians–going to give the Navajos the devil." At 3 p.m. that day, Sumner led his force out of the camp, three and a half miles from Zuñi on the road to Cañoncito Bonito. He left behind Sitgreaves and his unit (and, thus, Kern) but took the Engineer's escort, Major Kendrick and his thirty men, to help thrash the Navajos if possible and to build what would become Fort Defiance. Wrote Kern, "We have a prospect before us of remaining here for a couple of weeks or until Maj. Kendrick's return from the new post." Kendrick and Sumner did not return to the wagons and supplies guarded by Sitgreaves until the 23d of September, or possibly the 24th. At 10 a.m. of the latter date, Sitgreaves began his reconnaissance to the Colorado River by making a short, shakedown march of six miles.

Hardly was Sumner on his way to Cañon Bonito and Cañon de Chelly before he was almost killed. He rode his horse into a covered pit dug by the Zuñis to entrap Navajo horsemen. Its bottom was lined with sharp pointed stakes. Three Army sheep were impaled and killed by similar traps which the Zuñis neglected to point out to their new allies. Shortly after Sumner's close call, a soldier came running into camp shouting that the Navajos were on his heels. Rice was ordered to mount up and follow Major George Alexander Hamilton Blake in a charge. The "Indians" were flushed from their hiding place but proved to be wolves, not redmen. Rice found Blake an interesting officer, like the drunk, Thompson. Bennett, the dragoon with Sumner, described Blake as digging a "grave" in his tent each night that he was in the field. More likely, this was a slit trench for safety. His precautions were not entirely out of order; Sumner's command was closing in on the heart of the Navajo redoubt–Cañon Bonito, Cañoncito Bonito and Cañon de Chelly.

The terrain was parched and broken now. On September 2d, Rice's comrades had to dig for water in the dry bed of a river, possibly the White Water south of modern Lupton, Arizona. The next day, at a "jumping off place," it was necessary to lower the battery down a precipice but, at last, the men were able to rest for part of two days on the south bank of the Rio Puerco, the Little Puerco or Puerco of the West as distinguished from the other Puerco River, a tributary of the Rio Grande far to the east. Rations were short and Rice grumbled in his journal, "I was so hungry that I could of eaten a raw dog if he was only boiled."

The march was continued across the river to a night camp on the 5th at a site called Willow Spring by Sumner, in the area of Black Creek. After crossing wet arroyos and dry cañons, very likely Black Creek and its West Fork, the contingent marched until it could espy the huge dike of volcanic trap called Black Rock. This monolith marked Cañon Bonito. On the 7th Sumner reached the Cañon proper but marched right through it and on up to "bottomless" Red Lake. There he split his command. He left his supply wagons there, or in Cañon Bonito, and many of his men under Major Electus Backus. This New York-born West Pointer (1824) had performed gallantly in the Mexican War after Seminole War service and was a dependable officer. He was the son of a War of 1812 hero, Lieutenant Colonel Electus Backus, who had fallen mortally wounded at the head of his regiment in the defense of Sackett's Harbor. Assisting Backus in founding a new fort in the Cañon Bonito area were Lieutenant Henry Belt Schroeder, a West Pointer from Maryland; Major Kendrick, one of Rice's favorite officers; and Lieutenant Joseph Nelson Garland Whistler of the 2d Infantry. The Wisconsin-born Whistler had graduated from the Military Academy just in time to win honors in the Mexican War. After the war and garrison duty in Mississippi, he had pulled frontier duty at San Elizario and Fort Bliss, Texas, convoying wagon trains. Then came New Mexico service at Cebolleta, the Navajo country and Fort Defiance, where he became C.O.

When Josiah Rice's artillery company moved out of its Red Lake camp for Cañon de Chelly, it was shrunken to only eighteen men (the rest remained with Backus) and the diarist complained, "just enough to man the guns, to go to the Navajo country, and to lose our scalps." After marching about three miles, the troopers captured a well-mounted and well-armed Navajo. Passing an area of wheat and onions, possibly Coyote Wash or Crystal Wash, Sumner reached Cienaga Grande* on the 9th. It was a beautiful running stream, almost certainly the Wheatfields Creek of modern maps. Sumner pow-wowed with the Navajos, who were dogging his steps, near a height which Rice's comrades dubbed Saddle Mountain. When the Indians demanded bread and meat,

---

* In dry Arizona, *Cienaga* had more the meaning of creek or stream than its common meaning in Spanish of "marsh."

Sumner told them to make tracks. This they did, but not before warning him to stay out of Cañon de Chelly.

September 11, 1851, saw a skirmish near a stream which Rice took to be a tributary of the Cienaga Grande but which was, most likely, Cienaga Juanico or today's Tsaile Creek, flowing into Cañon del Muerto of the Chelly complex. Sumner ordered his hard-drinking dragoon, Major Thompson, to charge any Navajos he saw. Thompson did so and, like Custer twenty-five years later, found that he had charged too much and too soon. A band of Indians—Rice estimated that there were 1,000 braves—counter-attacked. Sumner had to quickly hurry Major Blake's company to the relief of the alcoholic dragoon. The *Diné* broke off contact without having hurt Sumner's command except for running off his commissariat. They took his entire herd of sheep except for six animals. It began to look like a hungry march to Cañon de Chelly. Exhaustion and thirst were also taking their toll of the animals. In two days, the command lost thirty horses. Rice claimed that 300 were lost, in all, during the great reconnaissance. Sumner had the animals shot by the rearguard to keep them from falling into the hands of the Navajo.

The soldiers found and followed an Indian trail down a cañon. Rice thought that it was a tributary to the Cañon de Chelly but it was almost certainly the same route which Simpson, Washington and Kern had taken in 1849, down Sheep Dip Cañon. On the night of the 12th, Sumner's little invading army was camped snugly in the valley itself, that is, in Chinle Wash south of Many Farms in another oasis of cornfields and Navajo hogans about a mile and a half from the mouth of Cañon de Chelly.

The Navajos' warning to Sumner against entering the sanctuary of the Cañon de Chelly, had been like a red flag to a Miura bull. He barged in, bullishly, on September 13th, firing off a few rounds of howitzer shell and ordering a rattle of small arms fire to dare the *Diné* to show themselves. Private Rice now had a look at the heart of Navajoland, which Richard Kern described thus, just two years earlier*. "It is very deep here; the rocks of sandstone alternating with strata of sand are sheer precipices of about 1,000 feet. The stream winding through seemed like a small thread . . . The rocks are sandstone, in some places perpendicular and in other shapeless masses. {We} found several cornfields and peach orchards. There are many lateral cañons and some of them of great extent. We measured what some supposed to be the highest point we had seen and its height was about 510 feet. We went into it about 9 miles and it became wider at every turn."

Heeding Simpson's old warning, Sumner placed flankers on each side of the cañon as he entered but once he had his main force on the cañon floor, he recalled them in order to bolster his force against a surprise attack. Of course, once he removed his sky-high flankers, the Navajos reassumed control of the cañon's rim. When Sumner reached the peach orchard near White House ruin, deep in the Cañon de Chelly, the Indians let fly with arrows, musket balls and rocks. The Colonel's answer was a hoarse shout to Rice's C.O., Lieutenant Charles Griffin, "Give them a shell!" Griffin needed no urging. The West Pointer (1847) from Ohio had been on scouting duty out of Santa Fe since 1849 and was eager to put his artillery into combat at last. The projectile fell short because the howitzer was hurriedly put into action without proper elevation. However, even though it struck the cañon wall some thirty feet below the rim it temporarily routed the attackers.

Rice estimated that he marched fourteen miles into the Cañon, doubtless investigating laterals, before the command was given to camp at dusk. After a late supper, Sumner reconsidered his position. The walls of the cañon rose above him to about 900 feet. His men's muskets could not carry to the rim, at least with any accuracy. Thus, Sumner can be forgiven for absorbing some of the nervousness of his men. Rice noted, "It seems the Colonel has changed his mind materially as we were marching in. It was, 'Take your time, Mr. Griffin,' but now it was 'Hurry up a little faster, Mr. Griffin!' " Rice was referring to Sumner's decision to pull out of the Cañon. The Colonel merely stated in his report, "As our firearms would not reach the Indians on top of the precipice, I thought it prudent and proper to leave the Cañon,

---

* "Notes of a Military Reconnaissance of the *País de los Navajos* in the Months of Aug. and Sept. 1849." Huntington Library Manuscript HM 4274.

which I did the same evening and, happily, without loss." Before they left de Chelly, the force was attacked from a willow-screened side cañon and Rice's shako was clipped —"I got hit slap-dab through my top knot and never touched a hair."

When camp was made on the Chelly River, or Chinle Wash, outside the mouth of Cañon de Chelly, Rice was so fatigued he fell into a deep sleep. When he was kicked awake by a non-com next morning, he found himself awash in his blankets. Too late, he learned that the whole valley floor flooded by night only to be dried up, by day, in the heat of the sun. Sumner rested his men for two more nights, then began his return march to Cañon Bonito and, eventually, Santa Fe. On the 16th, as they set out, Rice wrote in his diary, "Ho for Gila!" After eight miles of valley the men began to climb into piñon country which hid Navajo skulkers. The latter launched a dawn attack on the command, wounding the Colonel's orderly before they slipped away. They hit Sumner again at three in the afternoon but his rearguard killed one Indian and a dog, and the Navajos broke off contact.

Unfortunately, at this point Private Rice broke his narrative and remained silent from the 17th until the 22d of September, when he was camped at Rock Creek. He failed to mention the place or date at which point Griffin left Sumner's command, en route to Cañon Bonito, and began a hitherto unnoticed 1,216-mile reconnaissance to the Gila River and back at the same time that Captain Lorenzo Sitgreaves was making his well-known march down the Zuñi and Little Colorado Rivers to the Colorado and Fort Yuma. Nor did Rice suggest the route of march of his detachment after leaving Ganado Mesa area or Defiance Plateau, where the skirmishes presumably occurred.

On the 23d, when Sumner was already back at Zuñi, Griffin, Rice, *et al* were camped on what the Cannoneer puzzlingly called the headwaters of the San Juan! (Perhaps the St. Johns area of the upper Colorado Chiquito??) On October 3d, Griffin's detachment reached an area the men called Apache Plains on an "extremity" (tributary?) of the Gila, which Rice guessed was 71 miles from their destination, the junction of the Gila and the San Pedro Rivers. Two days march from Apache Plains brought the men to that point and a much needed rest of five or six days in the area of modern Winkelman and Hayden before retracing their steps. Rice visited a warm spring in the area before marching back up the Gila on the 19th through an area of Apache huts and cultivated patches of ground. Griffin's unit reached Night Creek at 2 p.m. of October 20th and, next day, encountered an opening in the woods which lacked grass or water. Thus, Rice was pleased when they once again reached "Navajo fodder" (corn) on the 25th. Apparently Griffin's command backtracked via Valle Bonito and entered Cañon de Chelly and Cañon del Muerto. On the 28th, Rice reported having passed "the celebrated Casa Grande–near {the} summit of Cañon de Chelly." (Rice later drew a picture of the *real* Casa Grande, near today's Coolidge, Arizona, to illustrate his New Mexico journal rewritten, apparently, from rough field notes but did not indicate whether he actually visited the ruin after the Griffin reconnaissance or merely copied the illustration in Emory's 1848 report.) On the same day that they passed this site–Mummy Cave ruin?–the artillerymen reached Wheatfields Creek again, where they half expected to find Fort Defiance under construction. But Sumner, of course, had finally decided on Cañon Bonito as the site. The next day, at two in the afternoon, Lieutenant Griffin led his reconnoiterers down into Cañon Bonito's unfinished Fort Defiance, to conclude an enormous march which has been completely ignored by historians of both the Army and the Southwest.

Regimental returns for September 1851 noted Captain L. Kendrick's detached service with an escort of two sergeants, two corporals, one artificer and twenty-five privates on Sitgreaves' California expedition until his return, September 2, 1852, when he took command of Fort Defiance. The only other off-post duty mentioned in the "movements" and "change of stations" section of the regimental returns is the hay cutting and cattle guarding of a handful of privates near Fort Defiance. Griffin succeeded to the command of B Company when Kendrick went on detached service, September 14, 1851. There is no mention of the fact that Griffin on that day was in the Chinle area and did not return to Fort Defiance until October 31, 1851.

Sumner's expedition of 1851 was no more victorious than that of his predecessors but neither was it the complete fiasco that some writers have called it. The Colonel was disappointed and defensive about it, himself, reporting thus to Washington: "We saw no Navajos till we passed Cañon Bonito. One of them then came to my camp and I sent a message by him to the two chiefs who were in the vicinity that if they would come to me with three of their head men, I would talk to them. They, however, refused and in pursuance of the instructions from the War Department, I ordered Navajos to be fired upon whenever they were seen hovering about. We killed and wounded a number of them but I cannot say how many. They never faced us or gave us an opportunity to inflict upon them any signal chastisement . . . My object was to attack the Indians if I found them in the Cañon and to destroy their crops. In this I was disappointed, there being no Indians {permanently} in the Cañon and but very little cultivation there . . . This expedition was not as decisive as I could wish, but I believe it was as much as I ought to have expected. It was hardly possible to close an Indian war of many years standing in one expedition. I believe the large post at the Cañon Bonito will, in a short time, effectively restrain the Indians . . . If this post does not put a stop to the Navajos depredations, nothing will do it but their entire extermination."

Sumner's major recommendation in tactics as a result of his march has been the source of some derision by historians. He urged the replacement of dragoons or cavalry with infantry! However, he had a point. The troopers could not fight from horseback; a cavalry charge in the

Navajo country was more than impossible, it was absurd. Army horses were unable to make long marches on the scant grass of the mesa and cañon country. The heavily laden horses always broke down. He suggested the use of a small body of "very select horse" and a larger body of infantrymen. This made sense. The horses should be led, not ridden, until contact was established with the enemy. Then he would have his dragoons mount up for battle. "A small body of this kind would be worth ten times their number of ordinary men on broken down horses," wrote Sumner.

Actually, Sumner's expedition (and Sitgreaves' and Griffin's reconnaissances) did awe the Navajos to some extent and on Christmas Day of 1851 Sumner and Governor Calhoun were able to sign a treaty of peace with them at Jemez. Recalled Sumner, "I told them (and they knew it to be true) that the troops at Fort Defiance could and would prevent them from raising a single field of grain unless they remained at peace. They promised to keep quiet and to restore all their Mexican prisoners and, as a pledge that they would keep faith, they gave up three hostages." However, Sumner felt that his rival, Governor Calhoun, had undone all of his work by handing out presents at Jemez. "These Indians will undoubtedly feel that their submission has been purchased . . . It would have been much better to have held them for a time with a rod of iron over their heads . . . I am by no means certain that this mistake will not jeopardize all the good results to be expected from placing a post (Fort Defiance) in the Navajo Country and I consider the mistake so important that I wish to make known to the Department my decided dissent and disapprobation of this measure."

Probably because of Sumner's initial optimism (later modified), Washington was most enthusiastic over his expedition and his new Fort Defiance. He had written to Adjutant General Roger Jones on November 20, 1851: "This large post is in the very midst of the Indians and cannot fail to cramp them in all their movements and it will harrass them so much that they will gladly make peace and keep quiet, provided they find that the post can protect as well as punish." The Secretary of War was enthusiastic in his annual report of 1852 to the President: "The benefits that were anticipated from the judicious arrangements made by the commanders of the 8th and 9th Military Departments have been fully realized . . . In New Mexico the depredations of the Indians have been entirely arrested. The Navajos and the Apaches, the two most formidable tribes in all that region, have been completely overawed and manifest every desire to be at peace with the whites . . . To Brevet Major General Smith and Brevet Colonel Sumner, in particular, much praise is due . . . The latter has not only succeeded in arresting the incursions of the Indians within his command, but has greatly reduced its expenditures."

The Commissioner of Indian Affairs added an amen in his 1852 annual report: "The Navajos and other tribes of this Territory, heretofore hostile and mischievous, have recently manifested a disposition to abandon their predatory habits and to seek support in the cultivation of the soil. To this end, they are anxious to be furnished with agricultural and other implements of husbandry.''

This rosy view of the Navajo situation was not shared by Private Josiah M. Rice, Company B., Second Artillery. His company had dwindled to a sergeant, a corporal and five privates. The latter had to shoulder axes as well as muskets. They were common laborers getting out logs for snug cabins to protect them from the coming winter. For six days a week they labored with blistered hands and aching arms and shoulders, on eighteen ounces of provender a day, until even the officers came to believe that they were the Lost Tribe. When no supplies arrived as week followed week, the men in the ranks began to urge the abandonment of Sumner's vaunted Fort Defiance before it was even finished. At last, even the Commanding Officer, Major Backus, was convinced. Rice made clear a little-known fact in his diary. Backus moved his force out, leaving a rearguard of forty-two men as a sort of forlorn hope. They were to hold the site as long as possible, then to spike the cannon and burn the fort before following him on his retreat to Cubero.

Whatever the records may say, Fort Defiance was abandoned by its commander. Luckily for the Army, New Mexico and Backus, the latter's battalion got no further than Hay Camp before an express reached him that a supply train was only two day's march from Cañon Bonito.

With Fort Defiance's future assured, Rice served there for a time, then was detached to escort supply trains. He visited Albuquerque, Tomé, Peralta, Trisco, Tesuque and Taos, while pulling this duty. (He and his comrades stole so much corn from the fields at Trisco, to extend their own meager rations, that the townspeople–puzzled by the strange unproductability of the season–ceremoniously marched an image of the Virgin Mary through the *milpas*, or cornfields.) He was back in garrison at Fort Defiance in 1853, finding his old friend, Major Kendrick, now in command. Even so, and with warm log cabins, and even theatricals to pass the time, Rice by now had had a bellyful of soldiering. He sought a discharge with the help of his parents and uncle. Kendrick tried to persuade him to stay on until he could make a long-promised march to California but Rice would not be swayed. On May 3, 1853, by Special Order No. 28, A.G.O., Private Rice received his discharge at Fort Defiance and became plain Mr. Rice.

In either Schuyler Falls or Elizabethtown, New York, Rice became a carpenter and married Mary Augusta Wood, of the latter city, on March 10, 1859. When the Civil War broke out, he was enlisted as a private by J. W. Flynn at Schuyler Falls on November 16, 1861, and was mustered by Captain Bankhead on November 29th. Rice was promoted to corporal in Captain Walker's I Company of the First Regiment of New York Volunteers, as of November 16, 1861. His enlistment was for three years or the duration of the conflict. The dark-haired, hazel-eyed non-com was stationed in New York City by November 29th and was promoted to sergeant on May 1, 1862. Stationed at Morris Island and Hilton Head, South Carolina, he worked in the saw mill and, especially, the paint shop. Rice was discharged on December 12, 1864, upon the expiration of his term of service and returned to Clinton County, New York. Shortly, however, he accepted an offer to superintend some Federal works at Beaufort, South Carolina. He and his wife moved there but, eventually (1869), migrated to Lansing, Michigan, because he wanted to grow up with a "Western" town. He bought a home at 320 North Larch Street and lived in it until his death at the age of 81 years, 11 months and 20 days, on November 27, 1914. The old soldier and G.A.R. veteran died of pneumonia. Just east of the bridge at 303 Michigan Avenue East in Lansing, he had set up a painting, decorating, glazing and paper hanging busi-ness. This firm's life of forty-five years ("J. M. Rice, House, Carriage and General Job Painting") made him locally famous.

Forgotten was the fact that Josiah Rice was, almost certainly, the last survivor of the great reconnaissance from Cañon de Chelly to the Gila and San Pedro, and back to Fort Defiance, in the fall of 1851. (Lieutenant Charles Griffin had died on September 15, 1867—more than 47 years before Rice passed away.) When Lieutenant W. A. Simpson wrote a history of the Second Artillery for the journal of the Military Service Institution in 1893 he said little, alas, of Rice's hard-marching old battery—"B was stationed at Santa Fe and afterwards at Fort Defiance, which post was commanded for some years by Capt. Kendrick, who showed marked ability in his management of the Indians."

EDITORIAL ACKNOWLEDGEMENTS

I would like to express my thanks to the following persons who helped me unravel several knotty problems in editing Josiah M. Rice's journal of a Campaign in New Mexico: Mrs. Alys Freeze, Head, Western History Department, Denver Public Library, who first suggested I edit this, and her staff; David M. Brugge, Hubbell Trading Post, Ganado, Arizona; John Neufeld, Michigan State Library; Mabel E. Deutrich and Elmer O. Parker, National Archives; Donald M. Powell, University of Arizona; Bernard L. Fontana, Arizona State Museum; Andrew Wallace and Margaret Sparks, Arizona Pioneers Historical Society; David Myrick, who drew the map; Opal Harber, who prepared the index; and, of course, my indefatigable typist, Mrs. Mid Rothrock, of Ross, California.

THE DIARY

Ruins of "
Pecas, Aztec, Church, N. M,

Campaign in New Mexico: Commencement

AFFECTIONATE FRIENDS AND RELATIVES

MARCH 8th, 1851

I THANKFULLY GAIN THE PRIVILAGE and leasure opportunity to gratify you with these few lines.

In the beginning of March 1851, I bade adieu to my friends in Elizabethtown, also in Plattsburgh, and pursued my way to New York, with the self-intention and friendly hopes of engaging myself as a comrade on a whaling or merchant vessel in hopes of bending my way to some foreign clime.

When arrived at New York, I intended {i.e., sought} employ in vain. All whaling merchants and dry goods merchants, having closed their applications, and not {having} opened {them for} the ensuing year, it was difficult to employ.

Being desirous in roaming more than in mind, and {on} the advice of a comrade so intended, in my residing hotel, I joined myself to the United States Army, during the term of 5 years to do and serve to my Superior Officer as he applied his applications.

The ensuing morning, after all applications being closed in binding me to the Force of the United States as a Soldier, to serve them in all their troubles and afflictions, I was taken to the recruiting depot on Bedloe's Isle.

When arrived at this soldierly palace, I considered myself out of companions' reach. But it was not long before one of the Lancer Sergeants came to my room to inform me to go to the Quartermaster's Office and receive my clothing, and take them to the tailor to have them altered, and then prepare for drill. Being short of a shirt, it was just into my hand to draw one.

After receiving my favorite suit of blue soldier clothes, I began to think of being a soldier, though I had not as much as thought of being a soldier before. But now I was a Soldier in good earnest.

The previous day, I was ordered to go to drill. I was, of course, placed in the awkward squad. The command was given . . .

> By the right flank, right face.
> By the left flank, left face.
> Front face.
> About face.
> Forward march.
> By the right flank; by file, left march.
> Counter march.

In this way, time passed away, with comrades I knew not, until our quarters became so crowded by new-comers that the oldest recruits were obliged to leave this Isle, and go to Fort Columbus, Governor's Isle.

Here, our bed was one of the finest yet known, or experienced, except once at home. Being out late at night with my companions, I was obliged to go into my father's sawmill (rather than awake my parents to unbar the door) and sleep on the soft side of a plank. Our bed was not the soft side of a plank here, but it was worse.

It was the soft side of the floor, which had been worn until all the knots were sticking up one inch above the level of the floor.

At this Isle, by lying on the hard floor and eating the coarse, clinging, food, I was taken sick with an awful pain in my head and bowels and forced to go to the Doctor.

Hearing many stories of complaints in hospital from the soldiers whilst in Old Mexico, and in fear of its being the same at this post, I overdone myself in sickness before reporting to the doctor, and at the time of reporting I was that weak that I was scarcely able to walk. I was sent to hospital, and here I remained until the 4th of April, in which time I had regained my health so that I was able to (scarcely) stand on my feet.

Gaining the information from my comrades that the detachment I belonged to was going, the next day, to ship for New Orleans, and go to New Mexico, to the 2nd Regiment of Light, or Howitzer, Artillery, and hearing of the ship *Juliet* being chartered and laying at anchor in the Bay off New York, my spirits enlivened and I informed the Doctor, or steward of the hospital, that I considered myself able to go with my detachment to New Mexico.

He informed the Doctor of my late proposal and he examined me and said if I considered myself strong enough to go that I could.

I took what few things my fortune consisted of, and endeavored to go to the garrison, a distance of one-half mile, but it was a fatiguing task before I reached it and if it was not for the kind assistance of one of my companions, I don't think I ever would of reached {it}.

As I came inside the Garrison, I found my comrades formed into two ranks, ready to march to the landing of the Ferry which we found in readiness to take us to the valiant bark. As I came to the ship, I found it quite a difficult job to raise myself, as I was very weak, over the bulwark or the high sides of the ship. On being directed where to go to find my bed, I endeavored to find it. I went into the hold of the vessel, where I found what was intended for beds for myself and comrades to sleep upon.

And what do you think they were? In the center as well as at each side of the vessel, were standards of scantling and cross pieces of inch and a quarter plank and, for bottoms of bunks, inch boards laid on the cross pieces, without nails or anything to stay them.

In this way, I was to gain my strength and on the sailor's coarse food, which is salt pork, or rattlesnake, as we so named it, and bean soup, hard bread and coffee, without milk or sugar enough to sweeten its taste.

We lay at anchor in this place until the 7th of April in want of God's will to favor us with a fair wind.

As I woke from my unhappy bed this morning and went on deck, I found the air in our favor, and the sailors busily engaged in drawing anchor and unfolding the gallant sails after which, in a few minutes, our bark was gliding over the blue waters and passing through the narrows of New York Bay, bidding adieu to that famous city which I never expected to see again. As we passed outside {of} the Narrows, we saw numerous vessels and steamships coming in from the sea. At night, the high bluffs of Staten and Long Isle were scarcely visible and the sun set in the sea and I retired to my soft bed.

The next morning, I arose from my restless night's sleep, went on deck, and looked for land. But my look was in vain when gazing over the bulwark and seeing nothing but the blue sea and a large steamship on her course to New York.

In this way, time passed away until the 12th of April at 10 o'clock a.m. I was standing on an extra spar belonging to the ship that was lashed to the bulwark at the lee side of the ship, to satisfy my desirous mind with the blue sea, when, to my surprise. at the distance of three-quarters of a mile, I saw something advancing, and rolling, and tumbling through the blue waters towards the ship resembling a shark. I informed the Sergeant there was a shark in sight, and the men overheard me and, in less than four minutes, the whole bulwark, cook galley, and bow deck were covered with anxious eyes in hopes of discovering something interesting to their anxious minds. As it advanced towards our ship, I saw there was upwards of three hundred of them, they came alongside our vessel, under our bows, and here they played until the First Mate prepared a harpoon and harpooned one of them and killed him on board. But the most astonishing thing, the instant the harpoon bled this fish, the rest dispersed and were seen no more. We opened the one we catched and he bled more than any beef ox that ever I have yet seen killed. His head to his fore fins resembled a pig in the plainest order. The seamen called it a Sea Pig.

And, in fact, I believe that it was one. It was dressed

and distributed among the ship's company and soldiers. I received a small share, myself, and it looked and tasted like beefsteak, as near as I can compare. The day passed away and the sun set in the sea and I retired to my unhappy sleepless plank bed.

April 16th. The 4th day passed away and all that came to relieve our desirous, and unhappy minds in view were the topmasts of some foreign vessel returning to her hopeful and happy home.

April 17th. This morning we were in sight of Abaco Isle, one of the West Indies. Here we see great quantities of flying fish, turtle and dolphin. The flying fish would rise out of a swell before our bows like a flock of jaybirds and fly into the next swell. These fish are of an average size from 12 to 13 inches in length and, as they were flying, resembled the river trout at home. The turtle is about four feet long and 12 inches thick, and of a light-green color in the water. The dolphin, as they swam along before our ship, were of changeable colors, sometimes white, again green, blue and yellow. The sailors catched four of them and they resembled in size, and color, the lake trout in Saranac Lakes.

April 25th .We were beating around Abaco in front of a fair wind 8 days. We had a fair view of the Isle, from one side. We see shipping lying in two different harbors. As viewed from our ship, the Isle was in large plantations. The first day we came in sight of the Isle, we saw a bark making her way to the harbor of Abaco. The Capt. of our Bark hailed her with a speaking trumpet. "Where bound?" – "Abaco;" "In cargo," "Slaves." The wind changed to our favor the 8th day and we were soon out {of} sight of this Isle The sun set in the sea, and I engaged myself in conversation with one of the sailors on the Bow Watch until evening, when, to my great surprise, {I was} to see, in the moonlight, the water before our ship foam and sparkle like fire.

I never as much as heard of this mysterious account before it came to my eye-witness. The bugle sounded the taps for all to retire to bed and I was compelled to fall in love with my soft plank bunk.

The morning of the 28th of April I was awoke from my restless night's sleep by the joyful hearts of my companions who were chasing up and down the hatchway, shouting the ship is towed by a steamboat. I dressed myself, went on deck, and found it to be the fact, but no land to be seen. I looked into the water and to my astonishment, as it had been as clear as a crystal, and now {was} as red as blood with the mud of the Mississippi River water. At 8 o'clock, we hove in sight of the levees or lowlands of the Mississippi.

Here we anchored and the pilot boat came alongside our ship. The Inspector came on board and inspected the cargo. We lay here until 5 o'clock, p.m., and drew anchor, and pursued our way up the winding course of the Mississippi.

We entered the levees as the sun was setting. At the mouth of the river we passed a brig and a bark laying on their broadsides on a sand bar. This was the first sight that had touched my eyes since leaving Isle Abaco. It soon become too dark to asertain what the surrounding country was comprised of and I retired to my soft bed in hopes of its being the last time.

April 29th. This morning, seven of our best men were missing, having jumped in and swum the river to escape. Enquiries were made, but no one knew, even the watchmen, where or when they had gone. The Major, Lieutenant and Doctor searched the ship, high and low, and also the steamer but they were wise enough to keep out of their way.

When I left New York, there was scarcely any buds of leaves on the trees, but here the oranges and lemons were in full ripeness and also sugar cane, tobacco, and cotton fields were to be seen as far as my eye could extend.

We reached New Orleans at three o'clock p.m. and anchored in the center of the river, the officers being in fear of more of the men deserting. A guard of men were placed all around the ship, and no sailor or citizen was allowed to come in a yawl nigh the ship.

Here we lay until April 30th in the after part of the day. The steam packet *James H. Hewitt* came to relieve us from the ship *Juliet*. It was astonishing to see our men when going on board the packet. The sailors' dinner was, as is the custom on this boat as well as all others on this river, sitting on the deck for the sailors to eat and, as the sailors were busily engaged in loading or taking our baggage from the *Juliet*, they had no time to eat.

Our men saw the dinner and you might see one poor half-starved fellow grab a handful of roasted potatoes and then another a handful of boiled rice and molasses and run away in fear of being seen. The Capt. saw them and could not help laughing as he turned away but said nothing except the next day. He gave the Major a joke of fetching starved hogs on board instead of soldiers.

May 6th. We were six days going from New Orleans to Jefferson Barracks, a distance of twelve hundred and 10 miles.

We had only one misfortune on our way. The 2nd day from New Orleans we had the misfortune to come in contact with an awful thunder storm which drove us on the banks of the river and blew our pilot house off. But immediate repair soon put us on our journey again.

Here, for the first time inside of 32 days, I put my foot on land. I was at this time as healthy and robust as any of my comrades. But as I came to walk I found it quite difficult to navigate on land, as I had become too used {to the sea} and {from} being sick when I shipped and {having} recovered on the water.

As we entered the garrison, the old soldiers, or Capt. Bragg's men, were lurking around the corners of the gate's passages to get a nick at us as we passed by. One old fellow sings out, "An Irish and, Faith! Jamy, what part?" One of our men replies, "Old N.Y.," but he was out of his latitude for he soon found himself in New Mexico.

May 9th. I am sorry to inform you that yesterday the most of my favorite companions left the garrison in search of that intoxicating drink that leads so many to their lonely graves. We were in search of them and we found some of them, unable to find their favorite home, lying under the trees in the lonely wood.

Orders were given by the Major for them to be fetched into the garrison, and kept in until sober. We found them all with the exception of seven who had deserted.

An escort of Capt. Bragg's Company was sent in search of them but their search was all in vain as they returned without knowing which end their head was on, in drunkness.

On the morning of the 9th of May, Major {Israel B.} Richardson chartered the steam packet *Arkansas* to take us to Fort Leavenworth. We were leaving the garrison as two of our men come in, and gave themselves up as deserters to the Major. As we came to the boat, the men were crowding into our pretended beds—a scaffold of inch boards—when the cross pieces of scantling broke, letting the best of 20 men and scaffold on 3 who were conversing with themselves underneath and broke one's back, squashed one's kidneys, and the other escaped without much injury.

The 2nd day I was taken with the cholera, which cramped me for 2 days and, with the will of God, after me recovering, one of my comrades was taken at night and in the morning, whilst the boat was wooding, taken, a corpse, to his grave.

May 11. This morning, we were within 50 miles of Fort Leavenworth. Today and the day previous, 9 of my comrades died in that unhappy pain. I endeavored to comfort them, but all to no use. It was God's will for them to die and when he calls on them, they must bid farewell to all things here below.

May 15, 1851. Last night we arrived, about 9 o'clock, at the landing of the Fort and were put ashore and compelled to lay down on the cold damp banks of the Missouri River to endure the night, which I found injurious to my (as well as many more of my companions') health.

In the morning we were received into the soldier's palace, or fort.

We were detained at the fort until the end of the month of May by sickness and the non-arrival of our cannon, which was daily expected from Springfield.

For some time previous and during our stay, every second or third day would witness the departure of long trains of Government wagons which, loaded with provisions, were dispatched with orders to push on as fast as possible to Bent's Fort, a trading post about five hundred miles on the road, there to await our arrival.

After numerous delays, on the 30th of May, 1851, we started on our long journey and not very encouragingly, for we left our Captain, besides several of my soldier-companions, ill at the fort and therefore went under command of the First Lieutenant.

This cast a shadow on our spirits as Capt. {H. L.} Kendrick was a great favorite.

The first day's journey was uninteresting as we only marched eleven miles and much of this was through the farm attached to the fort.

Our whole battery, embracing the pieces of the Company commanded by Lieut. {John Creed} Moore, consisting of two two-pound howitzers and eight long brass six-pounders, and to each of these, as well as to the caissons, were harnessed four fine dragoon horses. But many of these {had} never felt harness before and, at first, particularly, they gave us much trouble, and on the second day, when we came to and forded a beautiful stream running through a narrow belt of timber, we found it almost impossible to get our teams to pull together, and it was at last found necessary to dismount the men and have them drag the cannon up the muddy bank.

From where I stood on the opposite side, my attention was drawn to one of the prettiest *coups d'oeil* I ever saw. Below me, playing and kicking, were the horses attached to the pieces surrounded by the men. And on the opposite side, seen through the trees and shrubbery, were the rest of our company in their bright and gay uniforms, grouped around their shining cannon {and} appearing along the winding path which led down the high steep banks of the stream. The sun was almost totally excluded overhead and the warmth of coloring thus given to the scene rendered it truly beautiful.

When we emerged from this belt of timber, the first prairies met our view. The grass was high as the backs of our horses and grew so rank as to render it almost impos-sible to make our way through it except just in the road.

We found it sprinkled with flowers although neither so beautiful nor so abundant as I had anticipated. {They} gave it a pleasing appearance which we missed in the prairies that we afterwards passed. Perhaps it is one of the most beautiful sights in nature, to see a puff of wind sweep over these grassy plains, turning the glistening sides of the grass to the sun and seeming to spread a stream of light along the surface of the wave, like the surge at sea.

And a sight of these prairies would often cause {William Cullen} Bryant's beautiful lines to rise to my lips and I would picture to myself the magnificent plains peopled by the almost extinct redman, his leaving for a wider hunting ground, and fancy with the poet and his murmuring bee, that with

> The sound of the advancing multitude
> which soon shall fill these deserts
> from the ground
> comes up the laugh of children, the soft voice
> of Sabbath worshippers.

Here, by a mistake of our guide, we lost the California emigrants' path. But, on crossing a high roll in the prairie, we found out our mistake and after much difficulty got into the right road again.

About forty miles from the fort, the Kansas, or Kaw, River crosses the road and, on reaching it, we found a regular ferry established by Government and managed by two Indians.

This is one of the most beautiful rivers I ever beheld, and although but a quarter-mile across, it is very deep in some places, but clear as a crystal, sweeping rapidly along between high rocky banks and, at last, emptying itself into the Missouri a few miles above Independence.

On its banks near our camp, in a bark cabin I saw a beautiful and noble-looking Indian woman, a beauty of that order, who might command admiration rather than affection. Her fine black eyes shone as she observed our admiring gaze but she continued swinging her child, who was tied to a piece of bark hung from the roof by a thong of deer's hide, without deigning to return our notice of her. By the side of the cabin, on a freshly barked tree, were drawn with charcoal several Indian hieroglyphics. The whole scene, cabin, woman and papoose, staring at us with its large eyes, realized one of {James Fenimore} Cooper's lifelike Indian sketches.

We had hitherto been traveling what is known as The Military Road, and only struck the great Santa Fe road on the fourth of June at what is called Elm Grove.

We now considered ourselves fairly on the great prairies.

How discouraging the first sight of these immense plains is to one who has read the numerous glowing accounts of them. How far short they fall of these descriptions none can imagine who have not seen them; only covered with a short poor grass in some parts and in others producing nothing but a dry bushy plant or wild sage. They may be traveled over for miles and miles without finding bush or tree to obstruct or break the view.

In many places it is so perfectly level that you appear when passing over them to be traveling in the hollow of a mighty bowl. On all sides, the surface, although flat, appears to swell at the horizon while you are apparently climbing up the side towards that edge, which you never approach. But, Oh the breath of the prairie!

When the breeze—which always rises at sundown—fans your cheek after a hot day's ride, you sink quietly to sleep feeling that soft delicious air is breathing health and strength into your weary body. How much I felt this can only be known to myself. One of my reasons for going on this expedition, as I could have remained in Capt. Bragg's battery, was to obtain the restoration of my health, which had been for sometime very much impaired, and when I left Fort Leavenworth I hardly expected to get across the prairies alive. But I had not been 3 weeks on them before I felt that my whole being was changed and, ere I reached the settlements, I was one of the most robust of the whole Company.

At the Cottonwood Forks of the Neosho, where we encamped on the 9th, we were visited by a tremendous rainstorm which soon flooded the bottom in which we were encamped.

I can hardly imagine a more woe-begone-looking set of men than we were the day we remained here. All the morning, the rain poured down in torrents; not a particle of anything could we cook, but sat wrapped in our soaking blankets, in our little six-feet square tents, which by no means kept out the rain, but rather sifted it and made it more penetrating, while around each tent we had thrown up a small embankment which prevented the entrance of the water.

About noon, the sun shone and we heroes might be seen crawling, one after the other, out of our canvas dwellings.

At night, we lay down in our wet blankets on the muddy ground and, in spite of all the exposure, there were no colds complained of in the morning. Those of the city had been considerably sneered at by the country soldiers, (who called us the City Pets) prophesying that the effects of our previous indoor lives would not be seen {to be good}. But I can affirm you that we who have previously led what would be called by many a delicate life, had fewer cases of sickness and less shirking of duty than occurred among those young Hoosier farmers, whose whole lives had been spent in the open air, and of whom the other companies were formed.

The place we were now at is the same where the trader Chávez was so brutally murdered in 1843 by a party of land pirates. His grave lies just outside the belt of timber which skirts the stream. I, afterwards, while in Mexico, met with a young son of Chávez, about 11 years old, who had come to our camp to get medical advice for an uncle. In the course of conversation, we asked him (knowing that he had been educated at St. Louis) how he liked Americans. His little eyes glittered as he exclaimed, "When I am a man, I shall be a soldier, and then I'll kill every American I can. They murdered my father and I'll pay them for it."

Captain Kendrick arrived the night before we left this encampment. We passed, on the 8th, the Lost Spring, so-called on account of a remarkable difficulty in finding the exact spot where it rises.

As we were moving out of camp in the morning, a light rain, which had been falling for some time, ceased, and the sun shone brightly out. The heat of the rays seemed to engender from every blade of the wet grass countless myriads of a small insect bearing some resemblance to a gnat which covered us and our horses so thickly that the original color of whatever they alighted upon could not be distinguished. Without biting, they got into the nostrils, eyes and ears, creating a singularly prickling sensation and making our horses almost frantic with pain. After an hour's annoyance, a light breeze arose and swept them away.

We arrived at Pawnee Forks on the Fifteenth of June and found the stream so high that we were forced to wait until the next day for it to subside. This stream runs very rapidly between high steep banks, and any slight rain on the mountains will make it rise so high in six hours that the traders are not infrequently detained several days before it falls sufficiently to allow them to pass.

Here I first tasted buffalo meat. Our hunters, who were selected from the Companys each morning, had been successful in killing three out of an immense herd which we had seen crossing a roll of the prairies during the day. There must have been three or four thousand in the herd and from the distance, they resembled a shadow cast upon the earth from a black cloud as it passed across the sun. The buffaloes killed were two old tough bulls and a nice young cow, the latter of which Antoine, our hunter had taken. But in the general arrangement of making all buffalo taken from common stock we had to run the chance of our meat, and only part of one of the old bulls fell to us, which made Antoine so angry that he went to Colonel {Edmund V.} Sumner and told him he would, in the future, hunt for none but his own company. As this was not allowed, he hunted no more.

On account of the entire absence of wood here, we had to use the dry dung of the buffalo, called by the hunters *bois de vache* or buffalo chips, for fuel.

There was plenty of it around our camp, and it had one advantage over wood; it required no chopping. It makes a good and hot fire without flame, but has a strong ammoniacal odor, which is imparted to everything cooked by it. Our buffalo meat, which we simply roasted on the live embers, of course, partook largely of its flavor, supplying the want of pepper which our mess was out of. The part most esteemed by the hunters is the small entrails about a foot in length, and called by the delectable term, Narrow Gutts. These, although they were highly relished by the old hunters, never looked very inviting to me. To tell the miserable truth, I was much disappointed in the flavor of buffalo meat and would rather have a piece of good beef.

The buffaloes themselves have the ammoniacal smell I have mentioned. This probably may arise from the earth, which adheres to them after rolling in the mud where they stop. As the soil of the prairies is strongly impregnated with different salts, the mud holes where they roll, or wallow, become sometimes of very large size from these living mudscows carrying off, one after another, considerable quantities of the moist soil. The hunters call them buffalo wallows. The rain forms them into ponds, and fish are frequently found in them. Where do these fish come from?

A soldier from one of the New Port companies was drowned during our stay at Pawnee Forks. He received a prairie burial, wrapped in his blanket and clothes. He was placed in his grave and, without any form, it was filled up and covered over with stone to prevent the wolves from meddling with the body.

We found the Arkansas River, which we struck on the nineteenth of June, very shallow; and this is frequently the case with its tributaries. They are sometimes dry, and then resort is had to digging a well in the bed of the river in order to get water enough for cooking. It can thus always be found in abundance by going down two or three feet, and it is always clear and cool.

Although the northern bank of the Arkansas is well covered with grass and scattering groves of timber are not unfrequent, yet the southern bank consists of nothing but huge sandhills entirely destitute of vegetation. We had been traveling within sight of these hills for several days before we came to the river and could hardly believe that we did not see large cities on the bank. Indeed, we could plainly distinguish gilded domes of churches and roofs of houses. The deception was caused by the rays of the sun upon the pointed sandhills. While on our march along the banks of the river, a singular phenomenon occurred. Towards the middle of the day, while no breeze was stirring, we were met by successive blasts of heated air so hot as to scorch the skin and make it exceedingly painful to breathe. And these continued upwards of two hours. The sky at the time was entirely cloudless. But these gusts bore no resemblance to an ordinary current of wind, but rather to the blast of a furnace.

Although we had by this time arrived at the principal buffalo range, we saw but very few herds. The first sight of one of the animals at once shows him to be no easy customer to manage. The little glittering eye shines through the immense mass of long hair which covers the head and neck, giving the creature an exceedingly vicious appearance, while the contrast in size which is afforded between its hind and fore quarters adds materially to its hideousness, for he appears to be all head and shoulders tapering off at the very point of the tail. Their pace, which is called by the hunters loping, is very singular, being a clumsy sort of gallop but having the peculiarity of both fore feet being lifted off the ground at the same time, and then both hind feet, the same giving the animal the

motion of a ship in a heavy sea, first bows up, then stern. However, they manage to leave the ground behind them at a very rapid rate and will frequently outrun a good horse. The best mode of hunting them is on horseback and with pistols. A horse that has been used to the chase will bring you close enough to almost touch the side of the buffalo, when you easily kill him by a well-directed shot behind {the} shoulder blade.

At first, a horse cannot be induced to approach one of these animals, and will exhibit the utmost terror when brought within scent of them. But after a few essays, he is as fond of the sport as his master. As much depends on the truth of the first shot, a horse must know his business for by swerving at a wrong moment, he will cause the buffalo to receive only an irritating wound and, in that case, the character of the chase is changed. The creature at once becomes a dangerous assailant, losing immediately all his previous fears of man and rushing to the attack with frightful bellowings.

Large gray wolves abound in all parts of the prairies and in Mexico, and particularly about the Buffalo Range. They are generally seen in packs and will scent fresh meat or blood at a great distance and, being exceedingly cowardly, they never attack man, and unless driven by hunger, will not kill any animal, preferring dead carcasses.

It was almost impossible to get any sleep during the night after we had killed any cattle, as these animals would assemble around our camp and, sitting upon their haunches, howl in the most mournful manner all night long. Lieutenant Moore, having been obliged to leave a sick horse behind, one morning, sent back two men to kill him, about an hour afterwards, his feelings for his tired steed making him wish to spare him further suffering. When the two men reached the spot where he had been left, a few picked bones surrounded by a pack of snarling wolves were all they found. One night, while standing as a sentinel on the outer side of our horses at the Big Timbers on the Arkansas, I observed a man coming rapidly towards me tossing his arms widely in the air. I immediately leveled my gun at him, and challenged him, and receiving no answer, I was on the point of firing, when it occurred to me, that it could not be an enemy as no Indian would have acted thus. So I cautiously approached the man, who was now but a few steps off.

I discovered it to be one of our men, only partly dressed, and who had been seized with a fit, and was thus rambling unconsciously about. He had a truly narrow escape, as had I acted strictly by my orders, I should have fired. I had hardly got him to his tent and again taken my post when daylight began to show itself. I was leaning upon my musketoon, with my back to a small ravine along the edge of which my post extended, and my mind in a guilty reverie when, suddenly, from behind a bush, not three feet from me, a big gray wolf set up his dismal cry, unconscious of my presence.

It annoyingly took me by surprise. Snatching up a stone, I hurled it after his wolfship as he dashed precipitately down the ravine. I would have given something to have been allowed to shoot him. But as orders were to shoot nothing of less size than an Indian, I dared not alarm the camp by the shot. In one of the Newport Companies called by us Grass-eaters or Colonel Sumner's, two horses were shot by some frightened sentinel who had mistaken them for Indian warriors.

We saw but few Indians except at Bent's Fort. And here I should judge were less than ten thousand, and it was by introduction, secretly and alone, that they carefully avoided us. All these bands that roam over the prairies have a great dread of cannon. This will account for their avoiding of us.

They consider, and call, artillery "thunder and lightning instruments." A band of them, a few years ago, atacked a party of traders who, besides their rifles, were armed with a small two-pounder cannon, which was fired with terrible execution upon their assailants. This taught them to respect artillery and their fear has not subsided.

One evening, after encamping in a patch of timber, what was apparently a huge nest was observed in the top of a high tree from which all the lower bows had been cut. This, on close examination, proved to be a room constructed of buffalo robes among the branches, inside of which was lain in state the dead body of an Indian Chief, while under and around him were the finest skins, and embroidered dresses together with his arms and pipes.

The air is so pure and dry in these plains that Indian

bodies, thus posited, do not putrefy. On Chouteau's Island, two of our men found a dead Indian lying on the ground which, by means of sticks, they made to stalk about the Island to the surprise and terror of some, who were not aware of the motive power.

We passed by and over several prairie dog towns. One of these was very extensive, being three or four miles in circumference, and the ground shook under us as we crossed it with a hollow sound, as if we were passing over a bridge.

Although the name of dog is applied to those little animals, they bear no possible resemblance to our dogs. Even their cry is much like a bird chirp.

They are much smaller than generally represented, being a trifle less in size than the common rabbit, and far superior to the latter in flavor. Between the skin and flesh is a thick layer of fat which is a celebrated cure for rheumatism when applied as an ointment. We used it upon the backs of our horses, occasioned by the chafing of the saddle, and it cured them at once.

The old story of the rattlesnake and prairie dog associating together is now exploded, it having been proved that the former devours the pups of the latter and directly a snake takes possession of a hole, it is at once forsaken by its former inhabitants.

It was by no means an unusual occurrence for us, after a heavy dew, to kill in the morning within a quarter of a mile of camp more than twenty rattlesnakes, which having come out to imbibe the dew, had become be-numbed by the cold night air and, so, were an easy prey.

Our Captain awoke one morning with one of these reptiles coiled up against his leg, it having nestled there for warmth.

He dared not stir until a servant came and removed the intruder. I had now an opportunity of testing the truth of what I had heard, but never before believed. In the month of August, only, these snakes are doubly venomous but totally blind. An old hunter will tell you that the poison then is so virulent as to deprive the reptile of sight.

We encamped on the 29th of June, about 12 miles below Bent's Fort.

This was to be rendezvous for the Army of the U.S. and the first resting place since our march commenced. Hitherto we had a sufficiency of both grass and water for our horses and provisions for ourselves, but our guide had just come in and reported that beyond the Fort grass and water were very scarce, and Colonel Sumner, in consequence of the scarcity of provisions furnished for us, ordered that we should be put upon only half a pound of flour and 3/8ths of a pound of pork per day, each man.

This deprived us of coffee, sugar, salt, rice, etc., which had previously helped to make our provisions palatable. Now our meals will consist of dough of a simple mixture of flour and water, which deserves that name "{dough} fried in grease," or else what we used to call "slapjacks," this being a thin variation of the aforesaid dough, poured into a hot frying pan. Not very desirable fare, but we went to it jokingly.

On arriving at Bent's Fort, we found no scarcity {of Indians}, although we had seen but few Indians before. It seemed, as the buffalo were plenty in the vicinity of it, that they had assembled here for trading with Mr. Bent.

Major {Philip Roots} Thompson, a dragoon officer belonging to B company, who had been intoxicated from the time of leaving Fort Leavenworth . . . finding an Indian about his tent {and} imagining him in the intention of stealing, without hesitation went into his tent and got his whip, and gave the Indian four or five lashes. The Indian returned to his chief with his complaints and you might hear the warhoop echoing on the open prairie. One of our horses broke loose and ran into the Indian camp. A corporal and ten privates were immediately sent after it. On arriving at the Chief's tent, he ordered them away, saying he knew nothing about their horse, and if they came around his camp a'looking for horses, he would shoot them. Moreover, if they did not make haste away, he would kill them whetherso. The corporal returned with his few men to camp and reported the circumstances to Col. Sumner. The Col. exclaimed in a coarse tone of voice, "Very well, Corporal." No more was said about the horse until the previous (sic) morning.

We were all saddled up, tents struck, and wagons packed ready for marching, when Col. Sumner with forty dragoons marched with drawn sabres into the Indians' {camp}, taking the horse by his picket rope and led him out of camp.

We had moved out of camp and, as it was the custom of the Quartermaster to delay behind in camp to see if everything was taken and nothing left, the Lieut., going past the Indian camp to get to the road a near way, had a shot fired at him, and several arrows. On overtaking us and reporting the circumstances, we were nigh four miles away.

We had merely halted to debate upon the subject when an express came from the fort in great haste informing the Col. that the Indians were in full determine to take the fort. We marched out to the left of the road on the bank of the river and encamped. We had scarcely pitched our tents when an order was given to clean up for General Inspection.

At the first break of day reveille sounded and we jumped with joy with hopes of fighting.

In full equippage and in file, we marched within one mile of the fort, here halted and Colonel Sumner, with his guide and one hundred dragoons, marched into the Indian camp and called for the Head Chief. When asking them what they meant by such actions, the Chief replied, "Fight; although if you will give me one wagon-load of bread, another of coffee and sugar, we would say nothing about matters."

Col. Sumner, on hearing this, with a voice that would skin the reddest Indian on the prairie, said he might have his choice to leave the ground by 2 o'clock that afternoon or else he would give them a wagon-load of lead. Before 12 o'clock M.D., you might see them with a few deer hides and old crock to represent saddle, charging over the rolling prairie. We marched into the campground and there awaited their flight, but we had not long to wait.

Bent's Fort is so named after its owners, George and Charles Bent, who have long traded with Mexico and the Indians. It is merely a trading post for the latter and consists of a square of mud houses with a stockade around it. Here are kept the usual necessaries for the hunters, who come and sell the skins they may have secured in the mountains around.

These poor men are paid for their furs in goods at most extortionate prices. For instance, they are charged twenty-five dollars for a gallon of brandy while the New York price is two dollars.

These hardy fellows often, having collected a sufficiency of furs and buckskins, bring them to the Fort where, after bartering them off, they furnish themselves with a sufficiency of powder, lead, and tobacco for another six months' trip to the mountains, and take the balance in whiskey, with which they remain intoxicated as long as it lasts; and when it is gone and all applications for more, on credit, are refused, they cooly shoulder their rifle and start off to do the same thing over again. At Bent's Fort, we obtained a supply of draught mules to fill the places of the many horses that we had killed by fatigue on the march. Out of the hundred fine cannon horses with which we had started, not more than ten reached Santa Fe.

The Mexicans have always been justly celebrated for their dexterity with the lasso, and while crossing the prairies I had several opportunities of seeing a man in the employ of Bent, named Antonio, use it. He, having a well-trained pony, boasted that he could hold anything, even a buffalo, with his nicely-plaited lasso of deerskin which always hung at the pommel of his heavily silver-mounted saddle. In holding an animal after he is noosed, the principal skill lies in the horse who, as the lasso is fastened to the pommel of the saddle, unless very careful in properly bracing himself, will be overthrown by the sudden jerk.

One day an old buffalo bull passed near the wagon train and Antonio was told to show his skill on him. Proudly and confidently, he started and threw his lasso but instead of catching the animal by the horns as he should have done, he foolishly threw it over his head, this noosing him round his powerful neck.

The horse, seeing the lasso tightening, braced himself back and for an instant it was a trial of strength between horse and buffalo. But, the next moment, the bull was scouring away with the lasso, garnished with the silver-mounted pommel of Antonio's saddle, which had been torn off in the struggle.

Our time was too precious to allow us to linger here and on the seventh day of July, we again took up our line of march, leaving, just above the Fort, the Arkansas River, much to our regret, for on its banks we had always found sufficiency of wood, water, and grass.

We started this morning at eight o'clock, and were not out of the saddle until two o'clock the next morning and then encamped by the side of some small salt ponds, entirely without either wood or grass, and the water so brackish as to be almost unfit for drinking.

Our wagons not having come into camp with us, we, none of us, thought it worth-while to wait until their arrival, but all lay down to sleep, supperless. Never was anything enjoyed more by me than my sleep that night, except the next morning's breakfast. My bed, however, was only the ground with two blankets, and my saddle for a pillow, and my breakfast, salt pork and slapjacks.

I had not eaten anything since seven o'clock the previous morning.

As we left the fort, the Rocky Mountains began to show themselves on the horizon, and gradually became more distinct. We had seen the snowy cap of Pike's Peak, the highest point north of the city of Chihuahua, the day before we reached the Fort.

When we reached the foot of these mountains, I was disappointed to find them so entirely destitute of wood. They were bare with no real beauty aside from the grandeur inseparable from such enormous masses of rocks and mountain, and although a few are covered with small firs, we crossed but one of these.

While encamped on the Rio Colorado, after crossing the first or Raton Range of the Rocky Mountains, I witnessed the coming up of a thunder storm and, among them {i.e., the clouds} a sight not to be easily forgotten. We lay in a low valley while surrounding us were immense peaks. Slowly, on all sides, great black clouds came rolling over the mountains, seeming too heavy to float and sinking gradually down the sides.

At last, when nothing could be seen around but those black clouds shutting out the world from us, a long-arriving roll of thunder echoed through the valley and the gates of the heavens seemed to open on the mountains, for the rush of rain was almost confined to them— we receiving only scattering drops.

The first Mexican settlement was reached on the 13th of July, being a small village on the River Mora. It consisted of a few mud huts and was called Lower Mora.

Nothing could be more discouraging to men fated to remain a whole year in {New} Mexico Territory than the first view of this town.

The houses, or huts, were built half underground and consisted of but one room, roofed with logs. In one of them, I found a Scotchman with his yellow wife, and mongrel younguns.

He owned large quantities of stock and had several Mexican herders in his employ.

He had made himself comparatively rich by supplying trains and traders with mules and cattle. The few Mexicans who came around our camp did not seem to respect us. But they were swarthy, lean, and dirty, in a few rags, and with an old blanket around them, they were pictures of misery. The next day we encamped at a continuation of the same village, called Upper Mora. Here, the houses were a shade better, being entirely above ground, and several acres were planted to maize.

In this town, but a few days before we arrived, a party of Navajos assembled and killed three Mexicans, and taking away with them two unhappy children and one woman, besides several large herds of cattle, sheep and goats.

These Indians, or savages, are very strong and whip all other tribes, and come down off the mountains into those trying to live in Mexican towns and without their trying to defend themselves, drive away their cattle, sheep and goats, and even take away the inhabitants.

Expecting to have a fight on going through the pass, we prepared for it. The signal for mounting, called "Boots and Saddles," was quickly obeyed the next moment, and we filed out of camp in good order. At this moment, our Captain, whom we had left ill at Bent's Fort, joined us and, being deservedly a favorite, was received with hearty cheers.

All the other troops preceded us through the Mora Pass, and just as a turn of the road took them from our sight, our bugle sounded the toot. Supposing that our comrades were already engaged, we belly boarded our cannon mules into a trot with our sabres, and in a few moments, found the rest of the force drawn up in a battle array. We galloped quickly to our position in the center near Col. Sumner, who, surrounded by his staff, was standing on a small eminence. No enemy could be discovered by us, but after half an hour of suspense, our advance guard came in with the intelligence that the Indians had fallen back on the Pecos Pass, and would

there entrench themselves. We passed scattered houses, and small towns, until we came to the village of Las Vegas, on the Gallinas River, where it passes through an immense cleft in the rocks.

Here we encamped and, being on guard this night, I had laid myself down about twelve o'clock to take a small nap when I heard the sentinel near me challenge someone, who proved to be a Sergeant from our outposts with a prisoner in charge, who had been taken at one of the pickets.

I accompanied the Sergeant to Colonel Sumner's tent, where we left our prisoner. The stranger was a young and handsome Indian, and declared himself to be a son of the Chief Sandoval. This young man's object was apparently friendly, as he stated that he had come out in order to inform us that the Indians, which had numbered four thousand warriors under the Chief Carvajal, had been strongly entrenched in the mountains at Pecos Pass, intending to give us a warm reception but had disbanded the night before in consequence of some quarrel among themselves.

The next evening we stopped at San Miguel del Vado. At this place, but a short time before we entered, the same party of Navajos assembled and seeing a woman with an umbrella passing through the street, and not knowing the use of it, took it away, and searched the town, taking all away with them, without more injury. Here, for the first time in {New} Mexico, I see a grist mill.

A zaky {*acequia*}, or ditch, was dug. It commenced a

mile above town, to give it its head and fall, dug on the banks as high as water would run, and at the mill, a trough, with the two ends knocked out for a bulkhead and an upright water wheel, something similar to an old-fashioned tubwheel, and shaft running through bed stone, attached to runner, without either elevator screw or hopper, damsels or curb. But the tender sat by with his grain and, as fast as it ground, threw in a handful and in this way it was sure to come out either coarse or fine, or else not ground at all.

On the night of the 17th of July, we halted at Pecos. This is a small Mexican village that takes its name from the ruins of the Indian town which formerly stood here.

All that is left of what was one of the most celebrated of the Aztec towns is the church, which is of immense size, and supposed to be over five hundred years old.

This is the church which contained the sacred fire, said to have been kindled by Montezuma, with orders to keep it burning until his return. The fire was kept alive for more than three hundred years when, having by some accident been allowed to go out and most of the town having been depopulated by diseases, the remainder of the inhabitants abandoned this place and joined a neighboring village.

There are many traditions connected with this old church, one of which is that it was built by a race of giants, fifty feet in height. But these, dying off, they were succeeded by dwarfs, with red heads who, being in their turn exterminated, were followed by the Aztecs.

But a singular part of the story is that both the large and the small men were white.

The bones which have been dug from the floor of the church are certainly of gigantic size. A thigh bone that I saw could never have belonged to a man less than ten feet high.

While myself and a companion were examining the edifice, a mule that we had tied outside, having got loose, very leisurely walked in after us, apparently as anxious to satisfy his curiosity as ourselves and without hesitation went straight to the place where the altar had formerly stood. This was raised three or four steps higher than the body of the church. Up these walked the mule and, having reached the top step, he gravely turned round, and giving vent to his feelings and piety in a long "e'haw," as gravely descended and walked out of the building.

The day on which we reached Santa Fe, we passed through the defile in which we were to have been resisted.

On seeing the great advantages we should have had to fight against, we could only look at each other, with a stare-expression of "We are well out of it."

The cañon, or valley, in which the enemy were to have met us winds between high mountains for miles and then, after passing between two immense, perpendicular, rocky precipices, ascends and widens gradually for some yards. This is on a narrow shelf of the rock, only just wide enough for a wagon, the rest of the gorge being a deep rocky gulley about twenty yards across. Just at the top of the slight ascent in the road, the Indians, it seems, had planted themselves, having falled some trees and thrown them across the pass, thus occupying a raking position along it, there to waylay us.

The rocks on each side being too steep to climb, the only way for us would have been to carry the position by a *coup de main* and this, {force}, well-armed with rifles as they were, would have been no easy affair for us. In fact, five hundred resolute men could have defended the pass against twice our force. Towards the middle of the after-part of the day, we came in sight of Santa Fe.

Our first view of this place was very melancholy, for we expected this to be our soldier home. Although much larger than any we had seen yet, still there was the same mud walls and roofs, and the accompaniments of dirt, pigs, and naked children.

Here we found the Headquarters of the 9th Military Department, with D Company and I Company of 3rd Infty. and Col. John Munroe in command.

The City of Santa Fe, although spread over a large extent of ground, is very thickly inhabited and, with the exception of the buildings around the public Plaza, consists only of scattered huts surrounded by large fields of Indian corn.

On one side of the public square, which is of considerable extent, stands the Governor's Palace. It is the only building in the whole city having glazed windows. The Palace is a long mud edifice, one-story high, with a portico formed by extending the roof some distance over the street and supported by smooth trunks of trees.

This portico is also extended in front of all the houses facing the Plaza and it proved a comfortable protection to our poor sentinels in rainy weather.

The Palace has at one end the Government Printing Office and at the other the Guard House and Calaboose, or Prison.

On examining the walls of the smaller rooms, I found stuffed into holes, locks of human hair, with crude crosses drawn just above them and invocations to the saints. I cannot exactly account for these locks of hair, thus illustrated; but I observed the same thing in a wall in Santa Fe, against which it was said some prisoners had been shot.

Around the three remaining sides of the Plaza were small shops for the accommodations of traders who, when they arrive, immediately hire them to show off their goods to peddlers, who make this place their rendezvous. Indeed, it is this trade, solely, that gives Santa Fe its importance.

These shops are not exactly such as our merchants at home would choose to show their goods in, being without a window. The only light that the dirty sales room receives is through the door.

In the middle of the Plaza, a high mast stands, from which waves the American flag, while across the square is ranged artillery, embracing the guns belonging to us as well as the pieces belonging to Colonel {John} Brooks.

Fronting the Governor's Palace on the Plaza stands an old church, which was robbed of all its plate and furniture and ornaments some time before we arrived.

It is allowed to go to ruin, in consequence of this desecration. On each side of the altar is much fine carving and, above, there has been good painting but the rain has beaten through the roof upon it and nothing is now left but the head, apparently, of an angel, which is beautifully painted.

The date upon a tower in the edifice is 1768, but the church itself is much older.

Although there are four other churches, there is no burying ground, and the dead are enterred by the side of the road just out of the city, with simply a pile of stones, and a small wooden cross on the top of it. I did not witness any grown Mexican buried while I was in Santa Fe, with the exception of an officer, and he was enterred with military honors; persons of both nations following to the grave. But our troops had brought the measles with them and it was soon communicated to the children of the inhabitants, and carried off many of them. Therefore, funerals among the young were common.

In these processions, two men went first, bearing spades with which to dig the grave; next, music, consisting generally of a violin, and clarionet, played to some lively tune; after these come the bier, upon which was placed the body, generally without coffin. The latter, black with white tape crossed all over it, being borne empty, by two children across their shoulders, walking behind. The body was usually in its best clothes, strewed with flowers. And lying upon a white pall, the bier was borne on the shoulders of four children, generally girls, and after these come the friends, without any order, dressed in their most showy clothes, and most of them provided with a bottle of *aguardiente,* or home-made brandy.

After the ceremonies in the church were ended, the poor little innocent was buried by the roadside, and a pile of stones raised over it, and if the father was too poor, or lazy, to make a cross for his child's grave, he stole one from an adjoining stone pile. And the funeral party went home pretty tipsy.

The Mexican's houses, although very uncomfortable looking from the outside, are generally by no means so within, for, being well whitewashed, they look clean and are at all times cool.

The walls are built of large bricks of mud, called adobes, about two-feet long by one-foot wide and four-inches thick, and the mud, being mixed with fine-cut straw and dried in the sun, holds very well together if carefully handled.

These are built up with mud for mortar and very often plastered with the same substance, both inside and out. But, as the tools which are used are only a spade and a wood trowel, the walls are not generally very smooth.

On the top of these walls are laid young trees for rafters, upon which are again laid small sticks placed close together and over all a coat of mud from six to eight inches in thickness.

This roof, of course, is quite flat but the walls being built at least a foot higher than the roof on all sides, with holes here and there to let the water escape.

They prevent the earth from washing off, as the grass soon grows upon this roof, it becomes impervious to the water.

The floor is nothing but the bare earth, trodden down hard, and I can say, from experience, that it makes the hardest beds – rocks not even excepted.

The walls and ceilings are whitewashed with a solution of bone lime made quite thick and laid on by means of a buckskin. The houses are often whitewashed both externally and internally and the lime, being of a brilliant white, renders the room very light, although perhaps the only opening is at the door, or a little grated window about a foot square, no window glass being used.

The houses of the poorer classes only consists of one room, with generally a partition wall as high as the waist running almost across it, and around the walls are built broad seats upon which the blankets that compose the beds of the family are laid during the day.

At night, the children use these benches as bedsteads, while the rest of the family, consisting probably of three generations, sleep promiscuously upon the floor, in filthy sheepskins and blankets.

The better sort sleep upon sacks of feathers and in low trundle bedsteads, hewn with an axe, from the rough wood. As regards the people who inhabit the houses, it is a hard task to describe them. The children from the age of four downward are generally left entirely naked. This, however, occurs more in the country than in towns.

The women of Santa Fe, being mostly poor, are badly clothed and are very dirty, which does not add to the attractiveness of their ugly dark countenances. They marry very young, but do not seem to know what virtue or modesty is, and being almost the slave of the husband, who will sit day after day in the sun and smoke his *cigaritos* without offering to assist his hard-working wife in anything, are very fond of the attentions of strangers.

Those who have much white blood in them are pretty, but these are seldom found in the lower order, which number as one hundred to one, in proportion to the upper class.

The men are the meanest and most contemptible set of swarthy thieves and liars to be found anywhere.

The rich ones will cheat and swindle and the poor sneakingly pilfer anything.

The commonest class are generally dressed in cheap dyed goat skin pantaloons, and dyed of two different colors, which are dressed like our buckskin and are as soft. A course shirt, and a blanket of the same quality according to the circumstances of the wearer; a palm leaf hat, generally completes the dress. Shoes are a luxury, only worn by those who can afford them, being replaced by those who cannot with a piece of raw bullock's hide tied to the sole of the foot.

Among the better sort, the pantaloons are of cloth,

ornamented with stripes of colored goat skin, and they wear blue jackets with plenty of buttons, and a black oil-skin cover to their wide-brimmed hats, a hatband, orna-mented with silver, and a small silver plate on each side of the crown.

The pantaloons of all classes have buttons all the way down the outside of each leg which, however, are never really buttoned but allowed to hang loose, exposing a pair of white cotton drawers under them.

And, more to the south, all classes wear a red sash around the waist.

The part of the dress which at once tells the wealth of the wearer is the *poncho*, or blanket.

This, although called a blanket, is nothing like this article known among us by that name, it being without nap, and woven, according to value, in small or large patterns.

The common ones are only white, striped with black, and worth about a dollar, and from the latter price they rise even to two hundred dollars.

Some are really beautiful, and being of wool, show charmingly their brightly colored small patterns.

The good ones are almost impervious to rain and you may even pour water into the folds of the *poncho* and it will not run through.

They are all made with a hole in the center, through which the wearer puts his head, and as it reaches nearly to the ankles, both before and behind, it forms an excel-lent protection against weather, and when not so re-quired, it is thrown carelessly, and worn with an air, over the left shoulder.

Several of the good ones, costing from fifteen to twenty dollars, were brought home for counterpanes by our men.

However, this quality is only to be found on the backs of the Mexicans and a serious obstacle presents itself to many persons against possession, for there is an universal presence of vermin on the bodies of all the inhabitants and it is not unusual to see women and men stop sud-denly, expertly hunt, and a sharp sound announces to you a death, while, the next moment, they handle the fruit, or cheese, which they are offering to sell you.

The women wear, if poor, an undergarment without sleeves and one petticoat, quite short, and leaving the shoulders and bosom exposed.

A narrow but long scarf either gray, or black, called a *reboso* is brought over the top of the head, and across the face, leaving only the bosom, supplying the place of a bodice.

It is under no circumstance laid aside while the owner is awake, being used dextrously, even at times of work-ing, or cooking; never, however, allowed to come in the way of the occupation.

The women of the higher classes are very fond of wearing an infinity of petticoats, which can all be seen, one a little below another.

The Mexican women are the most graceful and boldest walkers I know, their step being always free, and good, and their carriage never too stiffly upright.

From being accustomed when young to carry heavy jars of water on their heads, they acquire a graceful oscillation of their bodies.

The jars I mention are of all sizes and, with the rare exception of a copper pan, now and then, are the only articles used to cook or hold water.

They are made by the Indians out of a very abundant brick clay, being baked of a red color and glazed only inside, are globular in shape, with a short neck and somewhat small mouth.

At all the farms or ranchos we found the dung of cattle pressed into large slabs, which we ascertained were, when dry, to be used to bake the jars.

These articles supply the place of metal vessels, as they stand heat well. Articles of metal are very scarce. I do not believe that there are two doors in all Santa Fe hung on metal hinges, they being made to hang on wooden pegs, the same with shutters to windows.

The food of the poorer consists of a sauce, made by mixing the powdered red pepper, *chili colorado,* with hot water, and eaten with *tortillas.* These are thin cakes thus made: The dry Indian corn is at first slightly parched, then ground on their mills, which consists simply of two stones. The largest, generally about two-foot by one-foot, and a few inches thick, is hewn out of the hard boulders which abound in this country, and are cut so that by means of two legs, they touch the ground at an angle of 55° while the meal is ground with the aid of the second stone, which is small and narrow and only as long as the other stone is wide.

In order to use this mill, the poor women go down on their knees, and working the smaller stone somewhat in the manner of a painter's muller, after much trouble, they manage to work the corn, with the addition of a little water, into a thick paste, which is rapidly flattened out by the women between their hands, into thin cakes of the size of a dinner plate, and about half as thick, when it is thrown on a sheet of tin kept hot over the fire.

The skill and rapidity with which the poor creatures flatten out this paste into such thin cakes are surprising. Never have I seen one spoiled or broken.

These *tortillas* are mostly of a light skyblue color, caused by the rind of the kernels of the maize, which is of all shades, from bright purple to a pure white, although the dark colors predominate and the mixture brings them to the blue.

These cakes are not very inviting to a stranger but to the Mexicans they supply the place of bread, as well as of fork and spoon.

They are very skillful with them for this purpose, and I have taken dinner with rich men, when no other implement for eating was used.

Another favorite dish is *tole* or rather *atole.*

This is prepared of various materials, mostly of the common meal.

However, to make it really good, it should be prepared

in an open vessel by heating a few quarts of milk, or water, and when it boils, stirring in a mixture of fine wheat flour, mixed with the meal of the small piñon nuts obtained from a species of the pine tree.

After being boiled a short time, it becomes very palatable, and a great satisfier of hunger.

When made with only water and corn meal, it is, of course, not so inviting, although by no means bad.

The meal of an ordinary Mexican man is about half a pint of red pepper with three or four hot *tortillas.*

This he has without variation all his life, many of them never tasting meat, while those who do, cook it only after it has been dried, or jerked, as we used to say, "after all taste has been jerked out of it."

Our wood was brought to us neatly cut in short sticks by Mexicans and packed on little donkeys.

These animals are very numerous, and you may often see moving along, with a short rocking motion, large bunches of hay, fodder, or other articles without perceiving anything to cause the motion except, whisking about behind, there will be a donkey's tail.

These animals are treated with great cruelty by their masters, who not only overload them but, going upon the old idea that "a donkey eats nothing," do not provide food for them.

Children ride them, just jumping on, and always sitting upon the hindquarters, and never on the body of the animal, using a small club with which they guide by thumping the creature on either side of the head.

This system of guidance does very well, until some green fodder, or other tempting morsel meets the donkey's sight, when all the thumps and thwacks upon the head avail nothing. A rider has no recourse but to slide down over the tail and, by means of force, push the animal away.

These creatures are never harnessed in any other way than by putting on a pack saddle to which is fastened the equally balanced load.

They are driven generally in numbers by one man on foot who, with a short stick, thumps or pokes any loitering ass, at the same time uttering "Tesh, Tesh," which sound comprises all the donkey's vocabulary answering for "Go ahead," "Stop," "Turn," etc.

The Mexican mules are very poor, smaller than those of America and are principally used for packing.

Their loads vary from two hundred to four hundred pounds.

The Mexicans, through carelessness, allow the mule's backs to become chafed with the pack-saddle and they soon are useless.

Occasionally, a fine riding mule may be met with, commanding an exorbitant price.

These poor animals, as well as the horses, often present a very hideous appearance. The mule, as he passes through different hands, is branded, and thus carrying his title deeds on his hide, each owner, on purchasing, stamps him with a hot branding iron, having a combined mark, looking most like a Spanish notary's name or a

Chinese character, and when he is again sold, the iron is again reversed, and the brand is put immediately under the former.

The first is called *fierro* and the second *venta*.

The first place for brand, the neck is used; and after that the hips and hind leg.

The production of the last *fierro* is sure evidence of ownership, and any ignorant person not having the *venta* branded underneath may probably lose his mule, as the former owner can again claim the creature.

Most of the riding is upon their small mustangs, or ponies, of which there is a great abundance. In the southern parts of New Mexico are many herds of them running wild, never having felt the control of man.

While on our march to the Navajo country, I suddenly came upon a herd of them and their action, while running from me, was beautiful.

One of them in particular, a small cream-colored stallion, who seemed to be the leader, lagged a little behind, and after taking a good look at me, galloped off, playing a thousand antics; then, after a few minutes, he would stop, and turning his head, would have another good look, when he would again bound off.

He was large for a mustang, and made me wish to have a lasso over his head.

The Mexicans, when they break in one of these, do it thus: Noosing the rope around the creature's nose, the breaker lets him bound to the extent of the rope, say from fifteen to twenty feet, when by a skillful pull, the horse is thrown upon his back.

After repeating this until the animal evidently understands that he is not free, the man gathers the rope up, and jumping upon the creature's back, using the rope by means of bridle, urges him on, with whip, heels and voice. He goes with the speed of the wind but becomes weary; is brought back quite subdued and, bridled, again ridden until he is covered with foam, being completely cowed.

These ponies are used only for riding, and, when equipped with beautiful silver-mounted bridle and saddle, they have a pretty appearance.

They are never over eleven hands high and, although well made, are not capable of great speed or possessed of much wind.

They, however, are full of action and can endure much thirst and hunger, thriving best on grass or fodder, than on corn and oats.

Generally, when a Mexican mounts a horse, it is upon very heavy silver-mounted saddle with large wooden stirrups.

Behind him and upon the haunches, and entirely concealing them, there is a large flap of leather, ornamented with silver studs, or covered with long black hair.

The Mexicans always arm their heels with large blunt spurs which they keep in constant action on the ribs of the animal.

I have seen these spurs with the rollers or rowels seven inches in diameter, and the shanks in proportion.

All rich Mexicans carry fastened to the pommel of the saddle a pair of shaggy goatskins, with embroidered leather trimmings.

These are used to cover the legs in hot weather, and hang from the hip to below the foot of the rider.

The bit, like the spur, is of the most cruel kind, so made that it would be a very easy thing to break the horse's jaw by a small pull, and hung inside of the mouth are loose pieces of copper, which keep it always sore.

Nothing could be better calculated than the whole equipment to ruin a horse, the sharp bit spoiling the jaw, and the heavy saddle and equipments destroying his back.

Every morning saw, collected along the southern side of the Plaza, an assemblage of ugly old women, trying to sell three or four eggs, a couple of quarts of goat's milk, piñones, watermelons, and molasses made from corn stalks.

When trade was dull they were actually employed upon the head of a youngster.

These ancient dames also sold the dry shucks, or covering of the ear of the Indian corn, cut into oblong pieces of three inches in length and one inch in width.

These are for making the eternal *cigarito.*

When neatly tied in bundles these skins are called *hojas.*

Every Mexican, male or female, carries at the girdle a pouch which contains a bundle of *hojas,* and a small bottle of powered tobacco, which is sparingly sprinkled in the shuck, and flintstone and tinder.

As tobacco is very scarce with them, they are not over-free to offer a *cigarito,* but when they do, they always first kindle it with the assistance of the mouth.

This, from their general use of garlic, does not improve the flavor of the *cigarito.*

I did not observe a single Mexican make any other use of tobacco and yet you rarely see either men or women without a *cigarito.*

Children, quite small, will go teasing their mothers with "Dáme un cigarito, mamá," and, on obtaining it, they sit down quietly and smoke with the most ludicrous gravity.

The universality of the *cigarito* is only equalled by that of their eternal game of *Monte,* played with cards.

The suits whereof are clubs, swords, and cups, and sums are delineated in their own proper colors and figures.

Each suit numbering ten cards, namely like the American from ace to seven, and then Knave-ahorse standing in the place of queen and king.

The mysteries of the game can only be learnt by losing at it.

The coolness with which the Mexicans win at this game is remarkable, their countenance never changing.

Men and women of all degrees may be seen sitting at the green cloth-covered table.

It is said that the priests also indulge at it, but I never saw one playing.

Sitting on the curb stones in the streets may be continually seen fellows without shoes, and almost naked, who, having scraped together a few coppers, are dealing *Monte*, with a greasy pack of cards, for the benefit of half a dozen poor wretches as ragged as themselves.

One day in Albuquerque, I gave a little fellow, about six years of age, a *cuartillo*, a small copper coin worth three cents.

The child went up to his mother, and holding up the coin, lisped out, "*Monte.*"

His gaming propensities seemed to have come upon him as early as his "*Dáme un cigarito, mamá.*"

Maj. H. L. Kendrick, receiving orders from the Commander in Chief of the Ninth Military Department, Col. E. V. Sumner, to join his command on the fifteenth day of August, we were forced to leave this lonely solitude to two companies, and Col. John Brooks in command, and proceed on our expedition to the Navajo Nation.

With the non-arrival of our horses and mules, which were applied for and not arrived yet, we were detained until the seventeenth day of August before we were able to proceed with our battery.

We marched out of Santa Fe on the morning of the seventeenth day of August, hauling our beautiful battery with us, consisting of one six-pounder field howitzer, one twelve-pounder field howitzer, two mountain twelve-pounder howitzers, also two caissons.

We descended the valley of Santa Fe Creek, nearly west, for five miles, when we left the Creek, and struck across a dry arid plain intersected by *arroyos* and dry beds of streams in a southerly course.

Twenty-three miles brought us to the Galisteo Creek which, at that time, was barely running. The bed of the creek is sand and pebbles of the primitive rock and lies between steep clay banks, traversed occasionally by trap dikes and limestone which, in one place, are so regular as to resemble a wall pierced with windows.

From this place to its mouth, there is scarcely the sign of vegetation. At the dry mouth of the Galisteo, and directly on the Rio Grande del Norte, is the town of Santo Domingo.

Before reaching Galisteo Creek, but after leaving Santa Fe some miles, a few sprigs of *grama* tempted us to halt and bale [some for] our nags but the principal growth of the plains was *Ephedra Diotis lanata (romería* of the Spaniards) *Nandecandia Texans.*

August 19th. Today we passed over and through numerous cañons and ravines and up steep precipices, one in particular, a ridge of sandstone rock averaging from thirty to forty feet in height, and about three miles long and, in many places, scarcely wide enough to allow our battery to pass. As we descended from these ridges, the Rio Grande came in our view, which appeared to be about three miles away.

As we expected to reach the Rio Grande by twelve o'clock when leaving camp, the principal part of the men had not filled their canteens, and its being very hot during the day, and finding no water on the road, the first sight of this river created a happy relief to the thirsty throats of my companions as well as myself. But being mightily deceived in the distance we were, many of us, nigh the act of famishing with thirst before reaching {it}, and I saw men offering one dollar for one swallow of water, and {it} not to be obtained at that price.

We reached the Valley as the sun was setting and found Col. Sumner and his detachment encamped on the bank of the Rio Grande, awaiting our arrival before continuing his expedition to the Navajos.

This encampment, although beautiful, lays about one mile down the river from the beautiful Indian town, Santo Domingo, which is inhabited by the Pueblo Indians, and supplies Santa Fe with the small amount of fruit which is consumed.

It has a very pretty appearance, every house being surrounded by small fruit trees.

Our time is too urging to allow us to linger here. And, on the 20th day of August, we continued our march down the winding Valley of the Rio Grande passing the pretty little village of San Felipe, overhung by a steep craggy precipice, upon the summit of which are the remains of a Roman Catholic Church, presenting in the landscape sketch the appearance of the pictures we see of the castles on the Rhine.

After passing numerous fields of maize and wheat, and adjoining ranchos, we came to the beautiful city of Albuquerque, a town of some size.

It has a fine church, although made of mud.

The residence of the *Alcalde*, Armijo, a favorite to all Americans, is here.

The priest's house, which I saw the inside of while on another visit to Albuquerque, is the best *(adobe)* dwelling I observed in the country.

The priests are high in position and always rich, but in morals and character they are, with few exceptions, even below their followers.

It is not unusual for them to have 3 or 4 wives, all living in the same house with them who, as well as the other people, manifest the most servile attention to them.

It really used to make my blood boil to see these poor wretches come into the room, where I might happen to be in conversation with the *padre*.

And, after kneeling down and kissing the hem of his garment, stand on one side, hat in hand, awaiting the moment when he might condescend to speak to them while the rascal was trying, with all his skill, to cheat me in the bargains I was making with him, not scrupling to tell the most abominable falsehoods if they became necessary to aid his plan. Even in the streets, the people will frequently kneel and kiss his robe as he passes them while he manifests outwardly no knowledge of the salute, passing on as if they had attracted no notice.

Our beautiful encampment (which was on the margin

of the River) bearing a beautiful grazing ground, Col. Sumner delayed his expedition for the purpose of refreshing our animals until August 21st at 3 o'clock p.m.

We crossed the Rio Grande del Norte.

After all was landed on the dry banks on the opposite side, orders were received from Col. Sumner to fill our water kegs for a long march without water.

We were busily engaged in doing what we had previously been ordered when Major Kendrick came riding up to us with the information thus: "My men, prepare yourselves for tramping without water. I know you have gone through many sufferings for the want of that element which moistens the body and gives strength to your weary legs. You have forty-five miles over mountains, and tremendous sandhills, and banks, to traverse, without the aid of water except what you partake, and carry with you. Therefore, fill all your water kegs, battery buckets, canteens, haversacks and valises and drink till you burst your bowels."

After leaving this beautiful solitude, we ascended the numerous sandhills without a road, except the narrow trail of the Navajos which we were scarcely able to follow by the aid of a guide. It was very beautiful to see our little army consisting of 3 companies, 3rd Infantry; 2 companies, 1st Dragoons; 3 companies, 2nd Dragoons; B Company, 2nd Artillery, besides 2 companies of recruits, and our provision wagons, of 33, drawn by six mules each.

We passed through and over numerous sandy plains entirely destitute of vegetation except, now and then, a bush of wild sage, until 12 o'clock at night, [when] we came to the not-running muddy Puerco River. Winding through a long clayey valley numerated with, now and then, a small patch of *grama* grass, and on its banks, overhanging its muddy bed, now and then, a few scattering cottonwoods.

On one side of this valley extends one of the most melancholy ranges of mountains, entirely of rough, craggy rocks without any real beauty, or either wood, grass, or anything to cover their desolate, ugly appearance.

This is the hiding place of the Navajos, who, when few in number, await for the gloomy night to descend upon the valley of the Del Norte and then take away the fruit, sheep, goats, cattle, poultry, and even the men, women and children.

After emerging from this low valley, we gradually ascended a long rolling prairie with, now and then, the abounding, craggy piñon tree and a few wild sage bushes.

About three o'clock p.m., we climbed to a ravine bending its way through a thicket of piñons and on its bank we found such a sufficiency of grass, it caused us to halt and graze our nags. In scarcity of water, we applied to digging a well, but all was in vain as the deeper down we dug, the drier the earth became.

As the sun was setting, the call for harness and saddle sounded and we pushed on as fast as possible until, at 1 o'clock at night, we reached (and halted and awaited till morning in want of daylight to find our mistake in the road) at the Sheep Springs.

Being extremely dry, and imagining we could strike the Big Bend of the Rio Colorado in a south direction in three or four miles, myself and 4 more of my companions took the freshest of our animals and struck off. We rode about 8 miles but found no water. We then turned back in worse humor than before, our hopes all in vain.

To the left of our halting place was a high peak of rocks, no less than three hundred feet high. This we had pitched upon for a guide.

But there being one to the right of the former, much higher than the other, we mistook this, which brought us to the Sheep Springs.

On coming to the spring, we found them surrounded by a large herd of cattle which had sucked all the water with the exception of a place the size of the crown of my hat under a rock.

In this place we satisfied ourselves and filled for each one of us a canteen. And then searched for the dim road, which our battery ahead made, which we soon found and followed up, and found the men lying beside their horses, bridle in hand, on the dry ground, fast asleep.

Which our feelings soon caused us to do the same.

On awakening at the sound of the bugle, I was very much astonished on seeing my horse with the snout of my canteen (which I had laid at my head) in his mouth, tipping it up in the air, drinking the water, {of} which he had not left me a decent drink.

About seven o'clock, we passed the celebrated Casa Colorada, the foundation of which is upon a high sand-hill. Surrounded by numerous *adobe* walls and the remains of large fields of maize, it has a very handsome appearance.

At 11 o'clock, we reached and encamped in the mouth of a deep long cañon multiplied by clear-as-crystal springs, and the refreshing grasses which our poor nags were in want of in abundance. As for wood, we were forced to climb the lofty rocks to find our supply.

In the afternoon, we reviewed our battery and gave it a slight polish. In case we should come into action it would show its smoking.

On the morning of the 23rd, we again took up our line of march passing through the before-mentioned cañon and over a rough, craggy limestone quarry, which we found very difficult for our provision and ammunition wagons as well as our battery.

When at the summit, in a distance, seen through the young numerous piñons and shrubbery situated on the sloping hill, under which bends the curling waters, is the beautiful town of Laguna (an Indian town).

It is one of the happiest dominions I have seen since passing the town above Albuquerque, Bernalillo. The people have a Governor and a *Padre*, and all a house and plenty sheep, cattle, pigs and corn and live in brotherly contentment.

The Mexican Government, in an ancient day, had established a church which remains, two bells hung by a thatch of cow's hide and another tied to the tongue, hanging down to the ground, on the outside, to ring by.

I entered several houses and always found them very free in placing before you their corn, pepper, bread, boiled onions and meats of the best they could afford and then, in a kind tone, tell you to *"Eatah!"*

The insides of their houses as well as the outsides are of a pure snowwhite, which makes them appear handsome. The women are very industrious. I don't know as I have entered a single house and found the women idle, being generally at work either grinding or parching (baking) the corn.

After receiving a fresh supply of forage at this town for our animals we continued our march up the winding cañon and valley, until 10 o'clock brought us to Cubero, and I was agreeably surprised to find it such a large and handsome place.

Their church is beautiful and most of the houses are high, and ornamental.

The inhabitants turned out to see us; and I beheld the prettiest girl I saw in all {New} Mexico, standing at the door of a meanlooking dwelling, in the main street.

Her complexion of marble whiteness showed delicately a slight rosy color in the cheek, while her large, beautiful, dark swimming eyes, with their accompanying heavy lashes and eyebrows, rested with a pitying expression upon me — for I was lying at the time in a wagon on account of sickness.

Oh, the beauty of the exquisite Spanish word *"pro-brecito"* (poor fellow), when heard from such lips — the sweetest of all sweet sounds.

The Mexican women in general are not handsome, for they commonly want the clear complexion which we deem inseparable from beauty's, but they have that large dark swimming eye, a lip usually high colored, and good teeth.

But the principal charm lies in their manner.

In entering a house, which you may do even though a stranger and be sure of a welcome of its owners, the *señoras*, without rising, offer you a seat and are ready at once to converse with you on any subject, and this with a piquancy and naivete exceedingly attractive to a foreigner.

It is a pleasure to meet some pretty *Doña* of your acquaintance after a short absence.

Wherever it may be, she immediately grasps your hand, draws you towards her, passes her arm around your waist, and presses you gently to her.

This habit of course, struck us at first as singular and rather forward. But the perfect nonchalance with which a lady-friend will thus press you to her heart, perhaps every day, soon shows that it is, in reality, only a common kindly recognition.

But the gusto and real grace with which two dirty old beggars will thus hug each other is a singular sight.

This mode of greeting is not confined to either sex.

The Navajos, previous to our arrival, had driven away all the stock belonging to this town, and left the people to rely upon merely the vegetation of the earth pertaining to what grew in its vicinity.

On the 25th we came to, and forded, the beautiful little stream Ojo del Gallo, which is one of the purest, clearest, streams yet seen in all New Mexico, being clear and running over the (seldom found, in this country) slatestone rock, while its banks are lined with the pure white coarse sand, extending to the very water's edge, and its flat bottom averaging twenty and thirty feet while its beautiful liquids gushing over its full breadth, twenty and forty inches in depth.

We now considered ourselves on the edge of the hateful Navajo country, although many stories had already arisen in relation to their powers and boldness.

Hearing they were well armed with rifles, pistols, and all well mounted and even armed with Mexican *cannon* which they had taken whilst in their terrible plunder in Mexico, and many of them well disciplined, we were truly in fear but they had become the rulers of New Mexico so perfectly that they had nothing to do but go into a town and supply themselves with what they wished most.

The word "Navajo" will create the most terror, and gloomy feelings, to a Mexican, you can imagine.

And go into a town and cry out "Navajo" and in a moment you will not see a single Mexican, all having rushed to their mud dwellings and closed doors on themselves for safety.

It was this report we used to make when wanting any fresh pork, chickens, mutton, and etc. when on a scout or escort.

When we had applied to our horses their fill, we again received the order by the sound of the trumpet – "Forward Battery."

Passing through the winding bottom of the Ojo del Gallo and across numerous drifting sand banks, which {were} fatiguing, it may seem to you sooner or later to see us poor gypsies dismount to irritate our poor horses which, harnessed to the guns, were striving their way through the belly-deep soft sands.

Seen on the right in the distant horizon, the ugly, craggy piñon tree surrounded by a few drouthless sage bushes, and the not frequent bastard red cedar, and overlooking those, was seen a range of the most gigantic ugly Black Mountains, apparently big and black enough to shake the earth around.

The first sight of this mountain would realize the most melancholy, desolate, lonely, gloomy feelings to the mind of a poor soldier (especially on the business we were) imaginable.

In this Black Mountain, I am told, the Navajos always resort, to resist themselves whenever in any entire danger, thinking the ugly looks of the mountain, itself, without their assistance will scare an enemy out of their country.

On our left were seen, the numerous tributaries of the Ojo del Gallo, lined with a range of (apparently abstructed {sic} by human hands) hills formed of clay and flat rock, varying from sixty to two hundred feet in height, apparently level on top, and in a true circle round. Sloped off at intervals, they had a very showy appearance in a long distance.

As we came around the base of a long black ridge of sharp-peaked mountains which we had seen before us for the last day's march, the valley became narrow and abrupt, with now and then the appearance of a volcano, or some ancient earthquake which, apparently, has taken the earth by main force and sat it on its beams ends.

Game in New Mexico is almost extinct, if it ever existed to any extent. Today, we have seen a few black-tailed rabbits and last night, while searching for my horse with my musketoon in hand, in hopes of hitting something that I might eat, as my appetite was extremely poor, I suddenly came, without the least thought in mind, not thinking to have an opportunity, upon a common Mexican deer.

But his sudden flight soon secured him from my eyesight and I had to look for game somewhere else.

Three miles up the valley before-mentioned, we encamped on a small eminence, surrounded with projecting and joining mountains, covered with red cedar and piñon, with, now and then, a few scrub oak.

In the valley surrounding our camp is plenty of the purest of genuine grasses for our horses and mules.

At this encampment I saw, for the first time since leaving the {Rio Grande} Del Norte, wild ducks, geese, and sandhill cranes, in large flocks flying over camp.

Extending through camp, on the north side, as well as the whole length of the valley as far as your eye could extend, was seen a ridge of volcanic rock, and eruptions, apparently created by fire. Seen between us and this ridge of lava, {was} the beautiful river Ojo del Gallo, running over the rough volcanic rock, overhung with willow and red cedars, rendering it truly beautiful.

Fishing was applied to this beautiful stream, and it was found to contain plenty of different kinds of fine fish, but the most bountiful were the burly river trout.

Our company officers, Lieut. {Charles} Griffin, and Bvt. Major Kendrick managed to catch enough of trout to keep them in fodder for three days without any other meat.

August 26th. This morning we proceeded on our march up the valley, passing, now and then, a pile of stones in small heaps, as though some poor man wanted to try his skill of farming on the Ojo del Gallo, but the Navajo would not accept it in their country.

On passing some remarks, insisting the cause, our Lieut. happened to pass us, who informed us that a party of American citizens were engaged by the Quartermaster in Cebolleta for cutting hay, and were sent to this place well-armed with rifles and one cannon.

But carelessness had allowed them to lock all their ammunition up in a chest, thinking not to have use for any of it. But the raging Navajo, in the deepness of their slumbers, charged on them and they were all killed with the exception of two men who were engaged in building a fire before they arose from their hay beds.

The two that escaped received several wounds, but in the gloom of night they hastened to the town of Cubero.

A scout of dragoons was immediately ordered out to bury the dead and secure what articles could be found.

On arriving on the ground they found one dead body laying near another there, with its scalp torn off. Graves were dug and, without any coffin, blanket, shirt, pants, shoes or stockings, the corpses {were} rolled into their holes and covered with dirt, and a pile of stones erected over the graves to prevent the wolves from meddling the bodies.

Three miles from this led us into an enormous plain, walled in with high mountains, apparently on all sides, whilst in the valley was seen pile after pile of volcanic eruptions, without the sign of tree, or plant, or any sort of vegetation, whatever.

On one side of this extensive plain, under a lofty mountain, (covered with a few piñon and cedar trees, and on the other side between us and the plain) was a ridge of lava that rough that I could scarcely look at it without trembling.

The earth here apparently has been in ancient days a beautiful level sand plain.

It seems the earth, from being strongly impregnated with coal and saltpeter, with the tremendous flames of fire, has burst the earth and left it in a confused state, leaving it sitting upon its edges, and in shape and color of a forge dross, or cinder.

Between this ridge and the mountain before-mentioned extends our road, winding along its range, which extends north and south no less than 70 miles.

It was between this ridge and mountain we had drawn our battery, one half and two miles, then crossed the before-mentioned rough ridge of lava, with much difficulty.

Winding around different ridges and cliffs of lava until 10 o'clock at night, when it became too dark to follow the narrow trail of the savages, we encamped under a high hill without water or wood except a small quantity we found on top of the hill.

Our night's sleep was very restless. In scarcity of grass, our animals, all night long, were squealing and whinnering like so many wolves.

We were forced, at the first break of day, in want of water, to proceed on our march again.

On the 27th day of August, we passed several herds of antelope, mountain sheep, deer, and snakes were variable, but as for horny frogs, {i.e. horned toads} and scorpions, the ground, as we passed along, seemed to move with their unnumbered flights as they skidded through the sands before us. Great signs of bear were seen but none espied.

In the vegetable line, I saw great varieties of cactus and different kinds of grasses besides the abounding Spanish soapweed, so called from the fact that the Mexicans use its root as a substitute for soap, for which it answers very well. Indeed, it is considered superior to it for the washing of woolens.

I believe it is rightly named the *lechuguillas*, or Spanish Bayonet, [i.e., yucca].

The singular shrub, which is to be also met with on the prairies, but where it never grows to any considerable size, consists of a trunk, very pithy, surmounted by a fine head of stiff leaves, each of which is about two feet and a half in length and armed at the end with a long thorn.

The leaves project from the stalk on all sides, and set as close as possible, and are of a dark green color.

The flower is white and very pretty.

As each year's foliage decays, it drops down against its trunk of a light brown color.

These dry leaves, when fire is applied, flash up like gun powder and burn with a bright light.

Our last night's march could be marked by their flame, which, as the night was cold, (although the days were uncomfortably warm), were cheering.

I have been thus particular in describing this plant for several reasons. One is its many uses of the leaves; of it the natives make their hats; also, when dressed like hemp, it is formed into ropes, and sacks, looking like the material known as Manila hemp, though coarser.

These plants have a singular provoking quality, being from two to eight feet in height, they will assume to the eye, in the twilight, the most deceptive forms.

To a sentinel, they will appear as forms of men, and many an unconscious soapweed has run the chance of a sentry's shot, from not answering to the challenge of, "Who goes there?"

If your mule or horse has strayed from camp and you start to hunt for him, in the gray of the morning you are sure to be led, first in one direction, and then in another, by one of these shrubs, which, from a short distance, has taken the form of your animal.

Time after time, you may have been thus deceived, yet never seeming to learn experience from a soapweed.

Another herb worth mentioning is the cactus which, when you are traveling through these enormous deserted plains, will often afford juice to quench your unknown (sic) thirst.

This herb averages in size from twelve to eighteen inches in height, and from eight to ten inches in thickness.

On its sides are ribs projecting out one or two inches, more than its former, which is well-armed with thorns to prevent it from injury. Also another species of cactus, which resembles the soapweed in many respects, is the *Neal Lattillus*.

Its leaves are nearly like that of the soapweed, being more clump and thicker, although the same length and color, and in the center of this bush as I may call it, grows a stalk, from twelve to thirteen inches higher than its suburbs.

On this stem is known that from six to twelve pears grow, which, when ripe, are of a yellowish color and taste much like a pineapple.

If you are on a tramp and fall short of fodder, these will serve the appetite the place of bread and meat.

And I learn from our guide, that he has known Indians to travel hundreds of miles without the aid of any other substitute except the fruit of the *Lattillus*.

During our day's march of August 27th, we passed over one of the beautifulest countries yet seen since leaving the United States, although the whole extent of New Mexico, of what we have traversed through, except just along the banks of streams, is of the most barren descriptions, being principally composed of a hard yellow clay so poor that, in most places, grass cannot be raised.

I have traveled more than a hundred miles without seeing sufficient grass to furnish my horse with a meal.

The roads, except in a few places where they happen to cross mountains or sands, are excellent, being as hard and level as a floor.

The land can only be cultivated just along the banks of the streams, and then the fertility of the soil amply repays the farmer, as the crops do not seem to exhaust the ground.

Many farmers work the same ground fifty years or more, without spreading upon it a particle of manure.

The seasons are also favorable to the husbandman; rain is, however, rare.

Before we left Albuquerque, which was in August, and another time, on an escort in January, the inhabitants were planting, and ploughing for the corn.

I have no doubt that were the Mexicans not so excessively lazy, they might produce anything they chose.

But when they have put their seed into the ground, they think they have done enough, and if it should not come up, and the plant thrive, instead of doing as they should – setting to work to remedy it – they simply "call on Hercules," in other words, fall upon their knees at the altar before the priest, tell him how unfortunate they have been, buy a blessing from him, and go home in blessedness.

The inhabitants produce maize, oats, wheat, onions, melons, grapes and several other fruits. I never saw any potatoes, although, as we know, it is truly said that the root grows wild in the southern parts of Mexico.

I have seen as fine melons, grapes, and corn in {New} Mexico as I have observed anywhere else.

And I have purchased onions as large as an ordinary-sized dinner plate.

Seven or eight miles march on our road led us into the most beautiful white pine openings ever seen by me, even from my infancy. The trees being far enough apart to allow a wagon to pass among them, and underfoot, the ground was perfectly level and smooth, except, now and then, a ridge of lava and the pure green grass growing ankle high. It was a beauty to the poor old soldier, but the Lord's curse, no water.

This is the rendezvous of all wild beasts such as bear, ass, catamount, wolf, deer, antelope, black fox, wild turkey, mountain goat, owl, American eagle, sparrow hawk, and a species of crow, besides scorpions, and horny frogs of all sorts and kinds, from a tarantula to a rattlesnake.

This being such a favorite game solitude, from its good prey, the Navajos also resort to this spot in fall and spring, for receiving their store of fodder.

We encamped in the 27th, afternoon, at the Cold Springs.

This place receives the name, Cold Springs, from its being extremely cold. At all times of the year, and especially at the time of our going past here, on August 27th, it was so cold that I could not sleep comfortable with four blankets, and a buffalo robe, although it is a beautiful place, being well-timbered with a noble growth of white pine, and a few scattering scrub oak.

Facing our camp on the south were enormous hills and mountains, extending to the very horizon, while below at the base was seen the beautiful gushing spring pouring its waters out of a long high poplar bush growing out of a pile of volcanic eruptions.

And around its base and along its winding stream which led down past our camp, was seen beautiful willows infringed with grasses of the lavish kind, which rendered it truly beautiful.

As we emerged from this encampment, we passed through a long valley, at least two miles long, while on each side were seen the abounding white pine and, in the valley, the beautiful green grasses growing at intervals.

Its beauties which matured in the mind of Col. Sumner made it a suitable pitched spot to establish a garrison.

Leading through pine openings while, now and then, crossing a ridge of the well-known *pedregal*, at last we came into a wide arid plain, covered with, now and then, a few piñon trees and, occasionally seen, an abounding pine, while around its trunk and roots were an enormous pile of black rock, and the surrounding prairies traversed with a few cactus, and the well-known *Lattilus*, and unknown sands, and at a distance across the glowing plain seen, making their best efforts for the wild, green wooded mountains, were enormous herds of deer, antelope, mountain goat, and the favorite wild turkey.

We had been drilling since twelve o'clock until about four, through a soft sandy bottom, creating a dead sensation to both us, and animals, although, as we came round a point of mountain, we saw our camping place. Oh, what a happy scene to the eye of a poor soldier! After a long, cold, and, perhaps, thirsty day's march, O, it will frequently bring to view the home fireside, when you come to get a small cup of coffee, nearly as good as pure water, a hot slapjack, and a small piece of boiled salt pork, nearly enough to just tempt your appetite, and go away in thanks for getting that much. How frequent I have witnessed those feelings is only known to myself.

Under a projecting rock with a large hole under its base, encircled by its enormous rock, we found sufficient water for ourselves and animals.

In the circle over the water, representing a pulpit, no less than fifty or sixty feet above the water, was plainly seen a half worn-out name, carved in the rock in Spanish, unknown to any of the natives, of which our officers, by its beautiful appearance in the shape of a dais, gave it {El Morro} the name of Inscription Rock.

It is a beautiful scene at a short distance and, on going around its base and climbing to the top, I was very much astonished, to find a large cañon in the center and large pine trees growing to the height of one hundred and fifty feet, and those not reaching one-third {of} the way to the top of its summit, while on each side of this cañon, on the flat of the rock, were the remains of two ancient towns so plainly to be seen that signs of adobe and stone walls, as well as crockery, was to be seen.

On making some inquiries in relation to this rock and towns, I learned from our guide, a Mexican, who has long been a *peón* or slave to the Navajos, that it once was inhabited by a head chief of the Montezumas.

A tribe of Comanche Indians resorted to take the town and kill the inhabitants.

The Comanches came in the night, thinking to find them in their sleep.

But as the custom of the town was to guard themselves from all other savage tribes by placing a sentinel over the town at night, alarm was given, and the inhabitants aroused to battle.

They fought six days and nights in succession, in the result of which the battle turned the sixth day to the Montezumas' favor.

The Comanches turned back to their former homes and troubled them no more.

The Montezumas, on account of the great loss of the many men killed in battle, deserted the town, and resorted to the Cañon de Chelly to rebuild again.

On the morning of August the 30th, we took to our road again, leading over a rolling prairie, with now and then a few scattering piñon trees, and a few bushes of cactus of different species, while on our left, at a distance, seen across the sandy prairie, a range of black, craggy, mountains extending to our lonely camp under the rock, while on our right you might see the plain gradually descending for miles, until it remitted itself into a dry sandy river leading east and west to where we expected to camp.

About three o'clock p.m., we came to a beautiful spring walled in with the primitive rock, its waters gushing out of the earth sufficient to turn a mill, while above us were the remains of another ancient dominion, formerly belonged to the same tribe, beforementioned, while in the valley between our encampment and the mountains, seen winding its curling waters, runs a beautiful stream overhung with willows and tall swamp grass bending down to the water's edge, and above us, erected across the stream, was a dam full of water which its liquids was found to contain plenty of fish, which by stripping and going into the water with a shovel our men managed to throw a sufficiency of them to give the whole company a good supper and breakfast.

This place by its numerous waters, receives by the natives the name of Ojo del Pescado, or Boiling Springs, {actually, Fish Springs. Ed.}.

August 31st, 1851.

By a false alarm last night, the whole command was aroused from their happy sleep, expecting to fight the enemy we had long been expecting to come in contact with.

But as the enemy proved to be a pack of wolves that came nigh to where some Mexicans were herding some mules belonging to the Sutler that was along with us, they, thinking it to be Navajos, deserted the mules and took leg Bale (sic) for the camp, with the before mentioned report.

It seems the mules, on seeing the wolves, joined with their crowd, became frightened, and had galloped away into the mountains a distance of three or four miles.

On account of our delay for the Sutler to hunt his mules, Col. E. V. Sumner proposed a muster by every Company Officer mustering his own Company.

The Sutler was successful in finding his mules and, about ten o'clock, we were on our line of march, with the whole command mustered.

Our march today is through a long valley, well watered, and grassed by the water from the Ojo del Pescado.

To the right of our road, in the valley three miles from our last night's encampment, is seen the ruins of an Indian town, said to have been built by the Puebbly {i.e., Pueblo} Indians, and called Zunia {i.e., Zuñi}.

But it seems a band of Navajos has descended upon the town, destroying the inhabitants as they retreated before them out of town, then returned and destroyed the houses.

After this sad catastrophe, the Zoneans {Zuñis} followed down the valley seventeen or eighteen miles, and built again upon a small eminence in the center of the valley, which is no less than five or six miles wide and, as for length, unknown to me, but no less than 90 or a hundred miles.

As we passed along on our road today, seen on the mountains was the general growth of timber. It consists of piñon, with, now and then, a lonely pine.

In the valley, however, there is no timber but a few wild sage and wormwood bushes, sprinkled with a few cactus.

During the day, I saw one of the largest birds I had yet seen in all Mexico, although this bird is well known among all Pueblo Indians as the eagle. All Indians celebrate this bird for his quills, which are the purest quality they can get in the country for feathering their numerous arrows.

And in most Pueblo towns, you may see no less than eight or ten of those birds sitting in a cage, with grates as large as your arm to prevent their escape, on the top of each Indian's dwelling.

About three o'clock in the after part of the day, we reached and encamped on the same stream of the night before with a scarcity of wood, but plenty of good grass and water for our poor nags, which were in great need of it.

On the morning of the 1st of September, we were visited by the Zuñi Indians, who were very happy to see us, it being the first time inside of six months that they had dared to venture out one mile from their town on account of the Navajos which, previous to our arrival, had driven away all their stock and destroyed their crops.

They informed us we were in four miles of their town, which was just beyond yon hills, pointing toward a ridge that extended from the valley. And on their seeing the smoke from our camp, and knowing that we were in pursuit of the Navajos, {they} had come to visit us, in our happy relief to them.

Our teamsters was soon ready for marching and we filed out of camp in good order, passing over the hills before-mentioned without seeing any shrub, whatever, to attract the eye.

As we descended into the valley, the ground and surface of the earth was covered with the remaining cornstalks, which was the only thing to be seen remaining after the destroyer.

About eleven o'clock, we reached the town, which is a handsome fortification, situated upon a hill. It has a beautiful appearance. At this place, Major Kendrick left his implements for his exploring expedition to San Diego, Upper California, also in addition to his implements he left thirty days' rations of meat, biscuit (which serves the appetite of bread), meat, coffee, sugar, rice, beans, vinegar, soap, candles, salt, etc. which our other rations are comprised of. Besides sixty days of the former, and then picked four of our men to leave in charge of {the rations} until he could go to Cañon Bonito with the sup-

ply train to pick his pack mules and men of the company to take to California with himself and Engineer officers, consisting of himself and four Engineer officers besides 32 men of my company, including non-commissioned officers and privates.

We now continued on our march over the wide and lonely, offended (sic), valley of that lonely and last town which we never expected to see again, as many of us expected to lose our topknots.

As our road was very rough, we only traveled three miles and camped under a large rocky ridge without water and a poor supply of wood. But as grass was favorable, our horses filled themselves very well.

At night, it rained tremendous hard and as myself and bunky {i.e., bunkmate} had no tent, as well as all the Company, we crawled under the limber of our gun, which we belonged to, to preserve ourselves from the rain. But as it poured down in such torrents as to flow over the whole surface of the ground, and there being a sloping ditch where the limber stood, the water came running into us like a river which soon routed us from that place in the midst of the storm, and in the morning sun, wrapped in a soaking blanket, were our men crawling around the fire to warm themselves, a more woebegone set of men you never saw than we were with our soaking clothes, wrapped in a blanket to keep the cold air from our wet backs. But it happened lucky for us, as the sun soon shone brightly out and, in a few minutes, we were as dry as ever, although I do not think the cold air would effect any of our well-trained bodies, as we considered ourselves case-hardened against storms and hardships.

On leaving this encampment, unknown to us the Zuñis had dug numerous holes, beside a deep ravine where the trail crossed, and placing in the center of them a sharp pointed stick, and over it laid a slight cover of dirt, to ensnare the Navajos.

Our Colonel, unknown to them, rode into one, and nigh killed his horse, and also, at the same time, our herder drove his flock of sheep into another, just below and killed three sheep, and caused us much trouble to get the remainder out. But we soon got out of this deluge (sic) and passed over a sandy ridge no less than sixteen miles, well-timbered with a fine growth of timber such as piñon, red cedar, scrub oak, with, now and then, a white pine and the well-known *Latillus* and cactus, while seen gracefully improving their greatest endeavors through the green wildwoods (sic) {were} a bounding deer and the long-eared rabbit.

But as I have not mentioned before, I will mention now there is two different species of rabbits, or hares, here, different from what we have seen before anywhere in New Mexico; one a small gray, with a black tail; the other, very large with long ears, looking like a mule, called a jackass rabbit.

In crossing a hill of sand during the day, the wheels of our battery and provision wagons sunk down to the hubs and the winds came sweeping the sands over us, as we were drilling along, seeming to want to bury us in its midst.

As the piece I belonged to was ordered to delay, in protection of the train of provision wagons, and with its long delay in the sands both myself and comrades in the hot sun was about giving up the ghost before we reached camp, which, on reaching, I found our men busily engaged in digging a well for water (as there was no water elsewhere) in the bed of a spring apparently where there had been a river.

I, in glory, jumped from my horse and ran to the place where they were digging in hopes of getting a drink to soothe my thirst. But my look was all in vain, on finding no water there.

I turned back, unsaddled my horse and picketed him on a small spot of grass where no other horse had touched. I had scarcely finished driving down the picket pin, when I was ordered to saddle up as quick as possible and follow Major {George} Blake. No quicker said than done. We took down the valley in which we were encamped, on a full charge, to where one of the soldiers had rambled after water and by hearing and seeing a band of wolves had, in a fright, mistook them for Indians, and came running into camp informing Col. Sumner that a band of Navajos had followed him in full jump nigh into camp.

We leisurely turned back toward camp until, off at one side of the valley in a ravine, I spied something in the appearance of water. On going to where I imagined

I saw it, I found it to be a hole seven or eight feet deep filled with plenty of the best quality of cool water for ourselves and animals, of which I drank a good fill, and gave my nag a chance, and then slowly returned to camp, and informed the Col. of what I had witnessed. On hearing my story, the Col. exclaimed in a coarse tone, of voice, "God spare you; you are the best man I have in my whole command."

The companies had supplied themselves with wood, and prepared for cooking without water. But the Col. soon had them saddling up to go to the spot I had before mentioned.

On leaving camp on September 3rd, we passed down a valley with, now and then, a few sprigs of wild sage, while on its side were lofty mountains covered with red sandstone rocks while, at its base, seen through the trees and shrubbery, were the pretended huts of the Navajos, now deserted.

These huts are comprised of the green bows of the abounding piñon tree, piled one bough on top of another in a circle similar to a pig-pen, with a gap in the front to go in and out at and continuing to carry up three or four feet high, and a slight bough roof, with a small fire in its front to keep the wolves and other wild animals out. It is the only refuge they have and will lay down at night and quietly sleep without the least trouble of mind or danger of being molested.

From this place, our road takes a turn to the right in among large sandhills and rocks; entirely much more difficult to get over than the ones of yesterday.

In this way, three miles fetched us to what proved a jumping-off place. As we were forced to lock all of our Battery's wheels and place a prolong, a rope from sixty to seventy feet in length with a large hook at one end and a loop or ring at the other, at each wheel, and also noose one around the muzzle of the piece, and thirty or forty men at each one of these, and with the aid of the mules, with much trouble we managed to get our Battery and ammunition wagons down the sloping precipice, a distance of three-quarters of a mile.

We were forced to remain at the base of this lofty precipice until the sun was enclosing itself in the gloomy shadows of darkness behind the western hills and {with} our provision wagons yet remaining at the summit of the lofty majestic hill, surrounded by two companies of the 3rd Infantry, and 5 officers, with Col. Sumner at the head, in command.

As I belonged to the small Mountain Howitzer Company, and the howitzers were at this time protecting the provision wagons, and Bvt. Maj. H. L. Kendrick had received orders from Col. E. V. Sumner to proceed on to the Little Rio Puerco, with the command, and there encamp and await his arrival.

With this order it seemed that the Col. had forgotten the detachment {to which} I belonged, as the Major, on seeing me, requested me to give the Col. his compliments and ask him if he would not be as kind as to let the two howitzers proceed with him to camp.

On hearing my request, with a coarse, long, and loud voice he exclaimed, "Certainly, my good man."

On hearing this, I instantly saluted him, made an about-face and walked away.

The Major proceeded, leaving the two companies of 3rd Infantry and Col. Sumner behind on the top of the precipice without a drop of water or, in fact, {in} short – none to be had in five miles of them.

There to endure the night and, the becoming day, to manage the provision wagons as well as possible.

We bent our course over a ridgey plain in the dark and gloom of evening until 11 o'clock at night {when} we reached and encamped on the banks of the not-running stream. But by the aid of the bright moon's beams, with much difficulty we, after a long time, found water in holes up the stream one-half mile.

But as I was exceedingly tired on returning, I stripped the harness from my horses and picketed them far enough away from the piece to not molest it, and immediately spread down my blankets on the ground with a bunch of sage bushes for a pillow, and soon dropped to sleep.

In the morning, the first thing that I knew, one of the men was pulling me out of bed, telling me to come with him to the holes for a camp kettle of water to get breakfast with.

This was right into my hand, as I had not eaten anything, since the day before in the morning.

And at this time I was that hungry that I could of eaten a raw dog if he was only boiled.

On the morning of the 5th of September, we continued our line of march, after two days' rest and all of our provision wagons safely up with us.

After crossing the river, our road bends off to the left through an enormous green mountain. {In} the notch which we passed through the piñon and red cedar trees were that close with their craggy limbs as to cause us much trouble and, many places, would scarcely allow us to pass, although we succeeded in going eleven miles and encamped at a small stream created by three or four springs overhung by large willows and swamp grasses under a lofty mountain covered with piñon. Col. Sumner named them the Willow Springs.

On the morning of the 6th of September, we struck off across a rolling country intersected by an occasional arroyo, and cañons with large, rough, red sandstone mountains extending apparently to the very sky, passing, now and then, a drove of mustangs, deer, and an occasional antelope.

And on the rolls of the prairies were numerous prairie dog towns. At last, we entered into a cañon with lofty mountains on each side winding to the right and left. Seven or eight miles led us into the open valley, in which we could, in a long distance of twelve or fourteen miles, see plainly a large black rock which is one mile from our beautiful fort, now in the center of *Valley Bonito*, and is well-known to the soldiers of Fort Defiance, as the resort spot for taking {in} items of the surrounding country.

(Also worth speaking of, Fort Defiance and Black Rock.

The first payday at Fort Defiance, on April 25th, 1852, as the soldiers could, by getting a requisition signed, get whiskey in the Sutler's store at six dollars a gallon, a return was sent in by Musician Thomas Tice for three gallons for to make a Fandango. The Fandango opened and went courageously on until about ten o'clock in the evening. Thomas Drumm, Assistant to Paymaster Clerk, opened two barrels of the before-mentioned return for, and got, the whole garrison intoxicated. The Officer of the Day called for the guard but found them all not able to roll over in drunkeness.

Mr. Musician Tice was sent for and asked how he got the whole garrison drunk on three gallons of whiskey.

His reply was, "Why, sir, I tapped the Black Rock."

And the password has been for the soldiers, ever since, when asked where they got their whiskey, "I tapped the Black Rock.")

We passed off to the left again passing across a rolling ridgey plain. Three miles fetched us into a narrow valley intersected by numerous sulphur springs surrounded by beautiful grass, the best yet seen on all my tramp even from Fort Leavenworth. It was up to my horse's back in many places and that thick that you could scarcely push through it.

September 7th

This morning we considered ourselves within one day's march of Cañon Bonito, the place where we expected to leave our provision wagons in charge of Major A. H. {i.e., Electus Backus} Backus and 1st Lieut. {H.} B. Schroeder, Bvt. 1st Lieut. C. M. P. R. Whistler {i.e., J. N. G. Whistler} besides Bvt. Major H. L. Kendrick and his party for San Diego, Upper California.

On leaving camp, Major Kendrick with the Battery and ammunition wagons took a straight line over hills and rocks for Cañon Bonito.

As myself was with the provision wagons again today, we were obliged to pass more to the right to shun or avoid the rocks and piñon thickets as much as possible and, being well into the valley, we were unable to see the mouth of the cañon, therefore passed it and had gone three or four miles before {we} made known our mistake.

When we galloped back and entered the mouth of the cañon, we found Col. Sumner halted with his command, awaiting our arrival. We marched through the cañon and encamped beside a small lake which our men endeavored to find bottom in, and all was in vain.

As we came into camp, our guide, who was much ahead of us, informed me that he saw a Navajo mount his steed and gallop over the hills at full speed out of sight. Also, on wandering around among the tall grass, which was quite equal to that of last night's encampment, we found a small patch of green corn and, in the center of a small mud hut no larger than a good sized hogshead, live embers with plenty of fresh corn cobs as though he meant to have one full belly before leaving.

On the morning of the 8th, we again continued our line of march, leaving behind us the whole company with the exception of eighteen, just enough to man the guns, to go to the Navajo Country, to lose our scalps.

Here was a parting hour among soldiers which never expected to see each other again. A part of the company to go on a scout, no doubt to lose our lives; another part to remain in charge of two guns at Cañon Bonito until our return; and the remainder to proceed with Major Kendrick to San Diego, Upper California. It was like in an enemy's country, shaking hands with each other, parting with father, mother, brother, and sister.

Oh, how it seems to part with a soldier-companion after two or three years servitude together in a land, so far from your parents; [it] can only be known to myself but, I can assure you, it seems like a farewell to the grave.

We now expected to find a sufficiency of hardships and fatigues, our provisions being packed on mules and no man allowed to take more than his horse blanket, with one shirt to change and one on his back, not having a change of pants, socks, shoes, although many of us had none or any drawers.

About 12 o'clock, we came to and passed a sloping hill one half-mile and, in many places, so steep that the gun I belonged to, in turning to our right and left down the crooked trail, turned over three or four times.

In a cañon below, we found a fine place of wheat and onions and, above, on top of the rocks, were numerous huts and in the valley below beautiful grass.

We now came to a stand in consideration which of these two places to establish a Fort, this or Cañon Bonito.

At last, it was decided that Cañon Bonito was the most suitable place.

This is a beautiful place, being on the side of a hill while below, in the Valley of Bonito, and seen across, are enormous mountains, and in a distance seen in the valley are numerous mounds at their base of which apparently is a lake of fresh water, while above us are the sloping rocks and carved cañons overrunning with the abounding piñon, underneath of which are seen, built up with rock and mud and covered over with logs and mud, the huts of the savage Navajo.

Up from this three miles was seen and taken an Indian, who, well-mounted, was found to have with him a bow and arrow besides a long-handled lance.

At night, we encamped beside some ponds and on our left were majestic hills, while on our right was the valley plumed with wild geese and sandhill cranes.

Our prisoner Navajo was taken up to the Col. who, on being asked by our interpreter how he came there, said he was looking at the men as they passed by and one of them ordered him to go with the rest and he was forced to come into camp with us.

On the evening of the 9th, we encamped on the beautiful little Cienega Grande. Today, by our crommeter (sic) we traveled 31 miles, and much of this over soft sands, in many places letting our cannon wheels in up to the axletrees.

About noon, we passed, by a deep crag, overhung with willows and red cedars, a rock representing a saddle, which some of our men named Saddle Mountain. On top of this was seen a ugly, dirty, set of men . . . seeming to want to speak with us. The Col. interpreted to them what they desired.

They replied they wanted some bread and meat. The Col. told them he would give them bread and meat, directly, if they did not make tracks from there.

They said they would give us enough if we entered the Cañon de Chelly.

The Cienega Grande is a beautiful stream. Apparently formed by springs, it bends its way through high peaks of rocks apparently reaching to the Valle de Chelly and thence onward while, rising apparently to the sky, are a range of mounds looking in the landscape sketch like steeples of churches and ancient towers, while in the valley are seen, now and then, a few white pine, and crags of piñon trees sticking among the rocks, and among those, now and then, an occasional cactus.

Game is scarce, although hares might be seen crawling in among the craggy rocks as our men were gathering wood at the close of day.

Our day's march today was very abrupt and rocky.

At the first break of day, we mounted and were not out of our saddles until it was that dark we could not see to go any farther, and then encamped in an extremity of the Cienega Grande. Without water, and being extremely tired from riding, none of us thought it worth a while to await the cooking of supper, but ate a few crumbs of sea biscuit – which our meals consisted principally of – and lay down to sleep, supperless. However, my bed at this time consisted of the ground with one of my horse collars for a pillow and my horse blanket for a cover; and my breakfast fresh mutton and coffee without sugar, and sea biscuit – a fine dish to eat out of your fist. But I can assure you we made the dry bones snap when walking into their affections.

We had now been traveling for the last two days among rocks and mountains and up steep cliffs and down craggy spurs in such dangers that you might often expect to see guns, teams, pack mules, and even men, go headlong down the rocks.

But the courage and coolness which our mules used to take when coming to one of these spurs is preceiveable (sic), many times climbing up hills that steep in many places that you might imagine them turning over backwards, and then with a pack as heavy as they could trot with on the level.

About 10 o'clock on the eleventh, we struck a belt of white pine trees with an occasional bunch of scrub oak which, in three miles, brought us to another tributary of the Cienega Grande while, on the opposite side, in the distance of two or three miles, was seen a band of Navajos in full attire for fight, and on fording, which we done by turning over one gun, Col. Sumner ordered Maj. Thompson, a dragoon officer to charge with the advance guard, of which the Navajos took flight to a flat-topped mountain on the right, of which in pursuit, another band of one thousand charged with their gray mustangs after our advance. And the Col. now ordered Maj. Blake to forward his company to his relief, which turned off to the left, and advanced. On one Indian's mustang horse going up the rocks (as he was in hopes), {he} was shot, and his horse run away with body tied to his back.

In the afternoon, by an approval of our guide, we passed to the right two or three miles and he led us into a deep valley which was numerated (sic) by corn, rice, onions, beans, with a few pumpkins.

As our provisions were short, you might see every man filling for himself a haversack full of green corn, another beans, or pumpkins, in order that they might have a good supper.

Col. Sumner thought our time too precious to delay there and we pushed on, many times in sand to our horse's bellies, and again on a solid rock foundation entirely without a tree, shrub, whatever.

In hopes of finding water, we kept traveling until late in the evening, in hopes, and, at last, was obliged to camp on a foundation of rocks apparently extending for miles, while in the eye-sketch there was scarcely timber or shrub.

Our poor horses were now in great agony for both food and water, as well as ourselves. Our horses {had} to rely to the solid foundation of rocks for water and grass which they had never done before. Since leaving Fort Leavenworth {they had not} been without a small quantity of either one or the other.

And ourselves without wood, or water, oh, as we looked at each other in pity, a camp of Death and, sure enough, it was a camp of Death.

In the morning, we commenced our line of march over a rocky surface of an enormous prairie, in a light sprinkle of rain. It was a happy scene to our poor horses as well as ourselves, as you might see the horses, as well as myself, when there might happen to be a slight hollow in the rock and a few drops of water gathered, kneel down and suck it up as though it was gold dust.

From our commencement of morning's march until the second day, our horses commenced giving out for want of water and in the course of the two days we were to the loss of thirty of our horses, as well as what the seven companies of dragoons were at, not numbering, in all, less than three hundred and no doubt if those had water {and} any grass again they would be good animals. But as they gave out, rather than let the Navajos have them, {the} rear guard, as they could not drive them, would shoot them down.

About 12 o'clock, we came to and crossed a small Cañon, no doubt a tributary of the Cañon de Chelly which, on entering, we were obliged to unhitch our cannon horses, and take them singly and lead them down the winding trail which the Navajos had formed by their numerous travel. And, on leading down our pack mules, which had died with the exception of two, being very heavily loaded, and {one} on making a slight stumble went headlong down the rocks, dashing itself into a slapjack and leaving our rations in a manner that did not look over pleasing in our minds, being very scant, and the few left with blood and dough, it was a horrible sight. But as for our battery, consisting of two small mountain howitzers, we were forced to unlimber them and let down first limber, then gun, and, in the same manner, pull them up the opposite side against a breast of rocks 29 feet high.

In the evening, we encamped in the Valley, about one and one half miles from the mouth of the Cañon. Here we found a sufficiency of corn for our horses, which you might see them smile as we placed it in the stalks before them and, as for ourselves, as the ears were in good roasting order, you might see each man, as he was gathering corn for his horse, have an ear in his mouth, running round from hill to hill like so many pigs in fear another one would get it before you, and being so extremely hungry, myself, I ate that much of raw ears of corn that I had no desire for supper when cooked, although our supper was but little better.

As for wood, we took the deserted wigwams of the Navajos, which were plenty around our camp, though for water we were obliged to dig for it in the dry sandy bed of the valley. But in digging 3 or 4 feet we found it plenty and cool.

Our small flock of sheep consisting (left from being stole the night before by the Indians) of only six, Col. Sumner ordered us to go and take our choice of one, leaving the other five to divide among the seven companies, a rather small portion for meat to last 3 or 4 hundred men one month. It was now we began to think we soon would have to graze with our animals.

The one selected for my comp'y was brought. Not being tied to the cook fire to butcher, {but} having been laid on the ground which appeared to be dead, whilst we were arguing among ourselves which as we had nine should be the butcher, up jumped the sheep and went capering through the tall grass in the bright moonbeams in the direction of the Cañon.

The word was the sheep is gone and you might see all of us, except the cook, running apparently for our lives, or a pack of starved wolves after a deer, after the sheep.

But in pursuit, as the sheep was about to enter the Cañon a man which we called Paddy (?), not having taken off his sabre, drew it and threw and pinned the sheep to the ground, sabre sticking through the sheep's neck.

In the morning, we had a general review and examination of arms and accoutrements and, after our horses were hitched in, 2 shots were fired from the cannon which {were} followed by the small arms to give the enemy alarm and warn them to battle.

As no Indians were in sight, we entered the Cañon in rather dull spirits, all of us expecting to lose our top-knots before coming out of it again.

Flankers were placed on each side of the Cañon in defense, to give us warning when seen coming the enemy.

In this way, we marched but a short distance, when we were forced to take in our flankers and send ahead an advance guard, and also one in rear.

In which five or six miles we came to an extremity in the cañon, encircled by the majestic walls or sides of which at this time in height no less than five hundred feet perpendicular, whilst below was a large town of ancient doom, formed by the hands of Montezuma, encircled by large peach trees, the limbs of which were bending with the ripening fruits, and surrounding those were large fields of maize, pumpkins, squashes, muskmelons, watermelons, one of which I found that large to serve the whole company of eighteen men.

We had not gone two miles from this place before, like the clash of thunder and lightning, came a shower of arrows, rocks followed by several rifle shots and then the sharp shrill voice of the Navajo while below, ordering us to retreat back from under the crash, was heard the coarse, grim voice of the Col.

Orders were received – "Give them a shell!" No quicker said than done. But as the Col. would not let Lieut. Griffin have his way, being in fear that we all would be killed in running the gun up close and bedding the trail, we just unlimbered without elevation and fired.

The shell struck apparently about thirty feet below and burst against the rocks, not touching one of them but reports were made by them afterwards that it scart eleven of them to death.

We marched under the before-mentioned clash fourteen miles and, with the closing of night, encamped under fears to march back in defense of our lives. Several shots were fired by us but proved that a musketoon ball did not go nigh the summit of the Cañon, which appeared to be at this time nine hundred feet high, while on the top were seen, appearing like so many crows in size and color, the Navajos, firing down to us with their heavily-charged rifles apparently like so many sharpshooters. Also you might see arrows coming down turning summerset {i.e., somersaults}.

Late in the evening, after supper was over, we received orders by the Lieut. to, without a whisper or jingle of a sabre, to saddle up ready for march. When all was ready the well-known voice of Colonel Sumner was heard in a whisper close by me. "Mr. Griffin, are you ready?" "Yes, sir." "Forward your Battery, then."

We slowly marched down the winding Cañon for three or four miles when I espied (as I was in the lead then and the Lieut. at my side, and the Col. at the Lieut.'s side) in the rocks, about four hundred feet from the ground, live embers of fire. I immediately whispered to the Lieut., "See that fire?" "Yes." "Do you see it, Col.?"

"Where? No, I don't see it. Hurry up a little faster, Mr. Griffin."

It seems the Col. had changed his mind materially as we were marching in. It was "Take your time, Mr. Griffin," but now it was, "Hurry up a little faster, Mr. Griffin."

We had marched about 8 miles when we heard, in a small cañon running into the main {one}, the barking of dogs and the pow-wow of the Navajo Chief calling his tribe to arms. Then, all was as still as death until we were opposite the cañon which was fronted with willow. "Whang, Whang, Whang" went the rifles followed by numerous arrows which a dragoon company fired in the direction of the flame of the rifles. They were a whole volley. I got shot slap-dab through my topknot and never touched a hair. But our Musician got a cut of an arrow on the left arm and one of the dragoon horses was shot through the neck. In relations to the Indians, it is more than I can say. But down opposite the peach orchard, in a hole in a large rock, the firing commenced again. But two or three shots soon put an end to it.

About twelve o'clock at night, we encamped at the mouth of the cañon on a low sandy bottom with a few humps of grass.

Being extremely tired, as soon as the command was given, "Picket your horses out," I can assure you I was not long obeying them. Took my horse blanket and coiled myself down on the ground, my head upon one of the before-mentioned humps which the stiff grass stuck into my hair and clinched me fast to it. This having no hesitation to the stopping of my sleeping propensities, I soon forgot all my troubles, slumbering in deep repose.

The first thing I knew in the morning, the Sergeant gave me a kick, saying, "Saddle up! We have to march three miles to a corn field." I gave a grunt and turned over, and found that I was lying in water up to my hips.

It seemed, in the night, the water run down from the wet sand and overflowed the whole bottom and in the course of the day the hot rays from the sun dried it up in the sand, again.

Shortly after encamping, we were in search after water to get our dainty breakfast. When, after a long search, it was given up that the only means was to dig. I was returning (whilst the other three were seated near the spot appointed to dig, with their arms in their laps) to camp to get a spade and when scarcely one hundred yards away, from behind a sand ridge was fired three shots, the balls of which tore the dirt up at my companions' feet. They jumped and run with cocked muskets to where the shots soared from and saw four Indians, riding at full gallop about half a mile away, and 2 shots were fired to help them along.

At this camp, we supplied ourselves with large quantities of green corn, beans, ground cherries, peas, etc., which our meals hereafter will consist principally of, as we have to rely to the wild prairies for our meat.

On the 16th of September, we again commenced our line of march for the Rio Gila.

We now expected to see a hungry day's march, and our small supply of provisions, furnished when leaving the wagons, were nearly consumed and destroyed, leaving us one quart of burnt coffee and 2 hundred pounds of hard biscuit, with about a half a sheep, depriving us of sugar, salt, rice, beans, vinegar, soap, candles, and, in fact, neither coffee or meat, merely a few weather-beaten sea biscuit.

The first, second, and third nights we encamped in the valley, but on the fourth day we had traveled all day long with the exception of 8 miles in the valley, through a thick belt of piñon, and red cedar trees, many times too close together with their sharp, craggy, dry limbs to allow our horses to pass side and side.

At night, we encamped in a small thicket-opening with very little grass for our animals, whilst on our left was seen a deep cañon and below, at its base, were large cold springs. Its waters which, as they rushed away, appeared like a river of fume, with a small, not frequently traveled, trail leading down to it, a watering place for the Navajos.

In the morning, as we were about to leave camp, a pint cup of the before-mentioned meat and biscuits was issued to us for our night's and morning meal.

We were all seated on the ground around the camp fire, awaiting to receive our new and favorite dish, when our Lieut. came to join our crowd to have a lick of it, too.

We were all seated with each one's portion, none having tasted it, awaiting the Lieut. to taste first, which, after asking for a spoon, it was the reply by the Sergeant, "There is none of our men able to have a spoon and most of them haven't as much as a knife." At this, the Lieut. took a sip from the cup, giving a smack with his lips and saying, "Shit, by God, shit."

These words had scarcely left his lips when I heard the sentinel that was posted at our backs cry the challenge of, "Who goes there?" Reply – "Friend." As orders were not to let any man pass outside of camp without having been passed out by an non-commissioned officer, the reply was to the friend by the sentinel, who proved to be Col. Sumner, "Stand, Friend; Corporal of the Guard, No. 32 . . ."

Those words had scarcely resounded when, like a flash of lightning, in the darkness of night at the back of the sentinel were the flash of numerous rifles, followed by numerous arrows.

The Col. turned from the Sentinel and run for his tent, which, with a light inside, appeared like a large bird ready to fly away, feathered with the numerous arrows. The Col. called for his Orderly but found that he was shot through the grinds, not able to move, moaning with deep agony.

Fires were put out and our horses fetched in line of camp with orders, "Sentinels all to be posted at once and all to sit down on post."

Two dragoon companies were placed outside of camp on one side and on the other and one at each end; also one of our guns, being loaded with cannister and primed, with the men sleeping at its sides, lanyards in hand, ready to pull at a sound of a rifle. We had scarcely prepared ourselves when in came another volley.

I was posted over the horses and, being exceedingly tired, on leaning against a hump of sage bushes I soon fell asleep. The first thing I knew, "whang" went the sound of a carbine, I jumped up, looked for my horses, which, on close examination, I found 2 of them had pulled their picket pins and were grazing in the edge of the woods three or four hundred yards from camp. I immediately led them in when one of the men from the Picket Guard came up from the cañon with a scalp, bow and arrow, large butcher knife, a lariat, war cap, and a small stick with several notches cut in it, no doubt the number of scalps he had taken, as it is the order with this tribe as well as all others when a man has taken so many scalps he is promoted to Lieut., then Captain, and so on, as he may improve with his bravery.

It was supposd that this Indian, as he had a lariat, was in the intention of stealing a horse, and happened to pass close to the guard where Sergeant Good of K Company, 2d Dragoons was with three men, in a thicket of scrub oak bushes. The Sergeant, being the only one awake, fired his carbine, which the ball passed through the pit of his chest. At this, the Indian resisted, to stick the Sergeant, when he drew his horse pistol from his waist-belt, and shot him again through the brain. At this, the Indian fell to the ground but strove to get up again. At this, the Sergeant took the Indian's knife and cut his throat, [from] which, in deep groans, he died. His scalp was taken off and his war cap was given to Capt. Dodds, a Volunteer Officer, who took it to Fort Defiance, and his bow and arrows given to 1st Lieut Whistler of I Company, 3rd Infantry who, I saw, had it, taking with him to New York.

As were about to leave camp in the morning, an Indian came down into where the dead body of the before-mentioned was and, piling a heap of dry brush over it, set it on fire and rode away unknown to us, until we saw the flames of the fire.

We had marched but a few hundred yards when we saw 4 Indians riding in the direction of our flanker. 8 dragoons was ordered to his assistance which, as they charged, they saw upwards of 2 thousand just make their appearance from behind a sandhill, then turn back in silence.

About 3 o'clock, orders were received – "About, charge! The rear-guard is attacked!" which, on turning back, proved that the rear-guard had shot an Indian and his dog.

On the 22nd, as we were marching along Rock Creek, we came to a long ridge of perpendicular rocks, which was an awful scene to us as we were forced to lead down our animals, then carry down packs and let our battery down against a breast of rocks 50 feet, which detained us for 2 days.

On the 23rd of September, we struck the headwaters of the San Juan, or St. John (sic). This is a beautiful, clear-running stream bending its curling liquids over a surface of round pebbles and through a narrow belt of cottonwood and scrub oak trees whilst on one side of camp is extended an enormous mountain extending to its outlet, apparently, and on the other side, back of our camp, is a horrible drifting sand plain which we have been marching across for the last two days.

In the morning as we were leaving camp, a light sprinkle of rain commenced but, to our poor beggarly wills, about 12 o'clock cleared off and left us a'smoking in the hot sun.

After two successful days march on the Rio St. Juan (sic) we took to our left for the Rio San Pedro thinking to strike it in two days. We took for our supply but very little water, which we all felt the want of, and many swore it would be the last day they would be without water, even if they had to pack it on their own backs.

At night, we encamped on a sandy prairie with but little grass or water but, as for wood, it was not to be found in the eye's universe.

Our poor mules and horses were screaming and howling in want of grass all the night long like so many crazy wolves, which made our Lieut. so angry that he swore he would gag the whole of them and I believe he would {have}, only for daylight soon showed its appearannce and left him no time, as we soon received orders to saddle up.

In the evening of October 3rd, we encamped on an extremity of the Rio Gila which we named, on account of a visit from the Apaches, Apache Plains. This encampment lies 71 miles from the Rio Gila. It is a noted grazing ground for the Apache mustangs.

Lined on the north side by a range of black rocks, while in its valley, which was covered with the glowing grasses, was seen our camp, formed of dragoons and artillery and frames of horses and mules and numerated by the almost-extinct Red Man charging, to show off their gray mustangs for sale, and {while} the bright sunbeams {were} pouring down its heated rays like the sharp points of so many heated needles. With the not-frequent tone of the jay bird, and the whistle of the magpie and, at night, to lay down on the evergreen carpet in the bright moonbeams, {it was} . . .

A camp of joy.

In the sixth day of October, we arrived at the junction of the Río Gila, and San Pedro, after having two successful day's marches.

The Río Gila, although very much like that of Río Grande, is a very beautiful stream, running through a wide valley, many places six and seven miles wide, and in more, not a mile from where we first struck it, is not more than three-quarters of a mile. But as we passed down it, it becomes wider and wider and at this camp at the junction, it is about nine miles wide.

Cottonwood and fir trees are frequent and the valley, in general, is well sodded with wild coarse grass, sand banks being not frequent.

The country in its vicinity is rolling and mountainous. I have no doubt, if it was once applied, that corn and many other grains could be cultivated to perfection, if it was not for the murdersome Apache.

And I have no doubt, in a declining year, you may see a fine and happy home to many a farmer who has not as much as thought of such a place in the known world, it appearing like a vineyard or many places in Mexico and the {Río Grande} del Norte.

I truly believe the whole country so far traveled and still south on the bottom of the Río Gila is swarmed with small black and yellow lizards which started from under our horses' feet in all directions. They moved with remarkable rapidity and it was difficult to catch them.

Their number was so great at times as to give a seeming living motion to the ground.

The Apache tribe is the most (with the exception of the Navajo) powerful of all the Mexican Indians.

It inhabits the range of mountains called the Sierra de los Mimbres which separates the State of Sonora from those of El Paso and Chihuahua, and on each side of this range is its extensive foraging ground, the country further east being under the control of the Comanches.

I do not think the Apache Indians are naturally brave but, having been long unopposed, they have become bold. So much so as to visit large cities amicably, and otherwise, in small parties.

The fact is, they so heartily despise the Mexicans that they say they would kill them all were it not that they serve as herdsmen to them; meaning this, that they them-selves neither hunt nor plant and, being of roving habits, they do not overburden themselves with cattle, preferring to descend from their mountain fastnesses and help themselves out of the first Mexican herd they come across, first killing the herdsmen if possible.

The latter have an instinctive dread of these Indians.

The word Apache is enough to make a Mexican herds-man tremble, although he goes armed with a sabre, carbine, and lance, and is always mounted.

One thing which has principally served to make this tribe powerful is the fact of one state frequently arming it against another.

Some tribes of these Indians live entirely on mule and horse flesh, while others eat the prairie wolf but there is no doubt they prefer fat cows and steers, frequently running off several thousand head at a time.

If a quarrel arises on the foray about the ownership of an animal, they kill the creature, leaving it where it falls, and, of course, the dispute with it.

Their track can be traced by this frequent mark of a quarrel.

A few miles to the south, a warm spring arises out of the sand between two small pointed mounds.

The water from its abundance forms a large stream.

The whole bottom of the basin, which is about ten feet across, is in motion from the boiling up of the water.

I passed my sabre down through the sandy bottom without the slightest difficulty and struck a rock about three feet below, apparently quite level and extending under the whole basin, yet, singularly enough, there is no rock visible around it for some distance.

This being an extraordinarily refreshing place for our poor nags, we, not thinking it a duty-bound order to proceed further, we on a numerous account of fine wood, grass, water and a noble hunting ground, considered it a right object to remain in camp 5 or 6 days and refresh our animals as well as ourselves, and lay in a stock of wild meat for our return.

On the 19th, whilst marching along the Río Gila, we passed by, and over, several great signs of once-cultivated ground, and further up near our last encampment, we saw in an opening encircled by red cedar trees several old Indian wigwams near the bank of the clear and cold water creek. Fronting those huts was the remains of several (woven out of willow) vats, which we judged were for catching fish with, as this stream, on fishing a short time, was found to contain an abundance of trout.

In the morning, as we were about to leave camp, I happened to come across a skull of an Indian.

Indian skulls may be picked up in many parts of Mexico and California and especially where Indians have once encamped.

Whilst at Fort Defiance, one day, as myself and a young German companion were exercising ourselves by a walk up a small cañon 4 miles east of the fort, we saw in the edge of the piñon brush a small pen three or four feet long 2 foot high and wide, covered with logs and dirt.

Which, on close examination, was found to contain the bones of about a half-grown person.

But the general way of burying is to pile a heap of dry piñon brush over the corpse and burn it.

Another time, on detached service, at a grazing camp 7 miles south of the fort, up on the top of a small eminence was a fresh grave, like a soldier's grave. But {by} the oddity of the head and foot stone set on the edge instead of the end we suspitioned it to be a chest of gold instead of a corpse.

Digging was applied by us and a German, who dug the first spadeful of dirt from the grave, being guilty, threw down the spade and said he would dig no more if there was two million. At this, the Sergeant catched up the spade, saying, "Go away, you feeble fellow. You never will follow the grave for a living," which, in two or three punches, he cut off some of the coarse hair with the spade.

Which came the perfume, and we all run for camp.

In the evening, we had nearly closed the corral upon our cattle when a pack of twelve or fourteen wolves passed right through among our tents and, seeing our fire, passed a few yards further in among the sage bushes and there commenced their howling. The fellow who had previously commenced the digging of the grave took his gun and was trying to slip up to them and shoot, when the sergeant took another and was trying his skill, when the former imaging him, as he was running, half-bent, {to be} the wolf, and fired shooting the hand which held the musket of a one buckshot, into his thigh.

No doubt, this terminated the grave digging.

Late in the evening of the 21st, we encamped in a small opening in the woods entirely without water or grass.

It was a pitying note to hear our poor animals which had been marching all day long from first sunrise through sand, many times to their knees, ee-hawing for water.

About 2 o'clock the previous day, we struck Night Creek and you might see the poor mules drinking apparently to burst themselves.

We marched along the creek 4 miles and encamped with plenty of wood, water, grass, and game, {of} which our men killed 2 fine antelopes.

Night Creek, although in an Indian country, may, in some day, be a beautiful, farmed country. The Apache now occupies its surrounding country as a grazing ground, although grass and large weeds grow and, whilst marching along the valley, we passed by several patches of wild grapes, hops, and a sort of vine currant.

And it was sport for us, on every few moments, to start out of the tall grass and weeds a species of large jackass rabbit and see them go skipping through, like so many deer.

A happy scene to us on the 25th {was} to see the Navajo fodder once more, as our meals had consisted (after our stores before-supplied at this place had run out) of leaving us a few sea biscuit and what meat we could kill on the road.

We now set to gathering the green corn, peas, and beans, and the pot was soon boiled, with the stamp of keep the mill a'going and then came the gathering of our little company of eighteen men with their little cups (with the exceptions of those who had none) ready to receive their portion of the partakable supper.

During our day's march of the 28th, we passed by the celebrated Casa Grande (sic).

This house is situated near the summit of the Cañon de Chelly and is said to have been built by Montezuma.

It has a very showy appearance, being on the top of a large, flat rock, and elevated some feet from the ground.

It has the appearance of being occupied by this tribe as a sort of rendezvous in defense, to war against all other tribes.

Its vicinity has a great appearance of the white man's axe, as but few others remaining in its neighborhood.

We had been marching all day long among rocks, and through thickets of piñon brush, many times, as I rode along, {almost} pulling my head from my body {and} making an exceeding hard day's march, in hopes to reach the wheat field, the spot before-mentioned, to establish Fort Defiance.

But on arriving late in the evening at the spot and finding neither wheat nor tents, we were shaded with a streak of horror, not having a mouthful to put in our mouths, even as much as a sea biscuit and, in short, not knowing where to get one. But its being a illuminated moonlight night, we wrapped ourselves in our blankets and endeavored to forget ourselves in sleep, when, in the direction of the fort was distinctly heard the roaring of a cannon, so plain that the Col. declared the Indians were at battle at the Fort.

In short, it proved the fact that, as we left the Navajo {country} into the Apache country, the Indians all resorted to Cañon Bonito {in} which they were nigh taking all of their stock mules and all, leaving them merely three oxen.

At 2 o'clock the next day, we arrived and found the commencement of the Fort at the mouth of Cañon Bonito.

Although of my company {there was} remaining left, after Major Kendrick's complement of men, only 7 Sergeant, Corp'l and 5 privates, now we were all obliged to shoulder an axe and musketoon and march to the woods to chop logs to build quarters in protection of the cold weather, which had began to impregnate with the warmth, and to defend ourselves against a tribe of tempting {i.e., tempted} savages which we knew not at what moment might attempt, which we were obliged, whilst the remainder were working, to place as a sentinel.

In this way we were laboring against our wills. And, at short, our meat gave out, then beans and rice, next sugar, coffee and vinegar. Next salt, soap, candles; leaving us mealy flour and water alone to rely upon.

But as only 18 ozs. was allowed for a man's portion per day, for a man to work upon it was a stinted ration.

In this manner, we were laboring for six weeks until it was given up that we were the Lost Tribe and that no provisions were coming to refresh us. And our right due was to evacuate the few houses completed and march to the Río Grande.

But it was decided by the Commanding Officer to leave forty-two men, rank and file, a part Infantry and remainder Artillery, to hold claims as long as possible, then spike guns and burn the fort, then tramp to the first settlements, at 270 miles distance, Cubero.

Major Backus began to pack his furniture, not knowing what to conclude upon. At last, he ordered the Battalion to pack. They left the Fort at 12 o'clock and, late in the evening, camped at the Hay Camp, seven miles distance.

Here was a camp of sorrowful hearts; the few animals had given out and left the starved drones or shadows of men to string out as mules and haul their bags after themselves.

But to God's will, shortly after encampaing, an express rode into camp, informing a supply train to be in two days' march of the fort.

Before this news arrived, you might see men in the woods among the piñon bushes, shacking {i.e., grazing on stubble} like so many pigs. But now, we could not eat our allowances.

Previous to this, the head chief of the Navajos had come in and declared a kind of treaty, which we took as we had not before, a great privilege to go a' gaining until, at length, the savage ran away with several men. At this, the Commanding Officer said if they did not let them back he would kill every Indian that came into camp. At this, no more men were missing.

In the closing of summer, orders were received that we must escort our own supply trains.

At this, a Sergeant and eleven men was amply ordered to march to Albuquerque and repair the road on our way and, when arrived at Albuquerque, report to the Commanding Officer.

When arrived, as the train had not showed its appearance, we were joined to the dragoons for duty until the supply train arrived.

In the evening before we reached Albuquerque, we encamped at the beautiful town of Tomé.

It is a large and handsome town, supported by its extensive vineyards, which add to the appearance of the place, being interspersed with melons, peaches, and fruit trees.

The vines are neither staked nor trellised, but grow to the height of perhaps four feet, perfectly straight, and, when at the height, spread out broad and bushy.

The grapes are very fine and of the Muscatel kind.

The most industrious part of the population is Indians; and many came to our camp with fruit.

The Indians are well-made, but seldom over five feet in height.

They are dressed in tunics of the same material as the Mexican blanket and wear what is called the Navajo *poncho*, so named from being made by the Navajo Indians.

It is of very fine texture with both sides alike and the patterns always in broad, black and white, stripes.

The women are singular objects; not over four feet in stature, with little round faces of a rich light-copper color.

Their dress consists of a tunic of blue or white, made quite full with a girdle at the waist and, being made very low at the neck without sleeves, only descends to the knees, while the leg from the knee downward is wrapped closely in several finely-dressed goat skins which end in a neat moccasin, all this giving them a singular yet pretty appearance.

The hair is cut short all round the head; and kept nicely trimmed.

Drawn together by the upper two corners and around their neck they wear what is called a *tilma*. It is a beautiful robe about three feet square, woven of black mule's hair with a showy edging of red.

One of these little women, with a basket of grapes, or peaches, placed upon her head, which apparently pressed her broad, good-humored face into a yet more good humored expression, and accompanied by three or four naked children, made a picturesque object.

When arrived at Albuquerque, several *fandangos* were called for by the soldiers.

The word *fandango* is only used when you wish to express a ball among the peasantry, and much fun is found at them.

The largest rooms are, of course, selected. At one end, carpets are spread, and all the women squat themselves on them, the men occupying the remainder of the room.

The most common dance is the *cuna*, which resembles our Spanish dance.

After all the couples are placed, the women begin a song as dreary and monotonous as a dead march.

The song keeps time with an old squeaking fiddle and banjo.

After each dance, your partner is allowed to find her way to her seat, alone, where she again squats herself down unless you have invited her to take a glass of brandy or wine – –a stall for the sale of which is always kept in an adjoining room, and where also is generally a *Monte* table.

At a ball *(baile)* of the higher class, the singing would, of course, be vulgar. But, generally, there are the squatting, fiddling, inviting and *Monte* table.

Mills are a great rarity when found but, in general, they are a seldom thing. In Albuquerque, whilst rambling around the town, off one side of the Main street where the *acequia* happened to cross, I heard a low grumbling noise which on going to it, proved to be a mill.

This was a curiosity.

What will our mechanics say to a flourishing mill built entirely without iron? All the wheels and other parts are of wood, of course excepting the mere stones, which are made from the ironstone boulders found in all parts of the country.

The flour ground by this mill was very coarse, the bran not separated.

Here I witnessed the fabrication of sugar from corn stalks.

The *Alcalde* owns the mill and boiling house, and the usage of this is paid in syrup.

The owner of the corn stalks assembles his neighbors and, proceeding to the mill, places the stalks, cut in short pieces, in a large wooden trough and each man, arming himself with a heavy mallet, soon breaks the stalks into small fragments.

Boiling water is poured upon them and then the mass is put into a hollow tree set upright in a trough. Into this, a plug is loosely fitted across which a long pole, fixed at one end, is laid, and all the young lever {it}. The juice is soon pressed out and poured into earthen pots built into the top of a large furnace kept burning night and day; women continually stirring the liquor until it is thick, when it is run into small clay moulds unless it should be wanted for molasses.

The workmen are repaid by an invitation to the house of the owner of the sugar, where they are regaled with molasses and *tortillas*.

In this way, these people help each other through the busiest seasons.

They were also getting in their wheat while we were here.

After being reaped and bound into sheaves, it is spread over a clay threshing floor in the open air and surrounded by high poles. Upon it are men with rude pitchforks made of limbs of small trees.

They throw the straw {i.e., wheat} into the air as oxen, driven round the enclosure, trample out the grain.

The poles keep in the large straw. By this means, it is broken up very fine but, being of no use to them, is not regarded.

The wheat, after being collected, is carefully washed by the women and children and then spread upon cloth to dry.

The agricultural implements are very crude.

Their ploughs are made of wood, without a particle of iron and, very often, in one place, which is in the shape of a three-pointed star with one of the points short, and to one of the longer ends is attached, by means of a rawhide rope, oxen, yoked by binding a long stick to their horns; the other long end serves for a handle, while the short one turns up the ground.

A rude heavy hoe and a common spade are precious things.

Hearing many stories of the pretty town of Peralta, in determination to see {it}, as 3 or four men were on business there for a day, I sent in {to} the Commanding Officer for a mounted pass.

Late in the day we arrived. It is upwards of six miles in length, situated in the valley of the Rio Grande, and from a half to a mile wide.

It is surrounded by extensive vineyards. The mode of cultivating the grape is the same as I have mentioned to be practiced at Tomé.

The valley here is the best calculated for the cultivation of the vine of any part of New Mexico, the soil not being too rich, and although there may be, now and then, a sharp frost, no snow has fallen here for years. You can well imagine how beautiful must be this valley when all the vines and fruit trees are in leaf and bloom.

The city and gardens are watered by numerous *acequias* or ditches, supplied by the river which is dammed up, a part, just above.

By means of these, the husbandmen are able to dispense with the aid of rain, which is scarce at all times in New Mexico.

Each field is provided with a small running ditch, and by cutting the bank, the water soon floods the ground. Each farmer has a day allowed him to use the water in this way, but cannot touch it at other times without the permission of the special *Alcalde* of *acequias* or, as we should term him, perhaps, commissioner of the water works.

This officer has the power of a judge of all things relating to his department.

Every person is required to keep his *acequia* in repair and, should any damage occur to his neighbor's property by inattention, the delinquent has to make good the damage.

One poor fellow told me that, in consequence of the frost, the side of his *acequia* had given away during the night and had injured a quantity of wine in his neighbor's house, for which he had been ordered to pay fifty dollars – a large sum for him, but his opponent was a rich man, and a friend of the *Alcalde's*.

As the supply train arrived and crossed the river, the mules were left in charge of us, to be taken to a grazing camp just outside Trisco. Whilst there, by some mistake, our men were kept two days without their regular supplies of food and, therefore, were obliged to forage upon the corn fields around, especially as the inhabitants had previously refused to sell any to us; and it had also been our constant habit to boil a pot of maize each night just before going to sleep and, sitting 'round the fire, to talk and eat.

The surrounding corn fields began to look rather unproductive, much to the astonishment of the natives, so, to remedy this, the figure of the Virgin Mary was carried around the fields in solemn procession – solemn, perhaps, to the poor Mexicans, but by no means to us.

The figure, which was very fantastically dressed, was carried by a woman in the same manner as she would have carried a child, and over them was held an old red umbrella, the only one in the village and reserved for great occasions like the present.

At the head of the procession walked the priest, book in hand, sprinkling holy water on all sides, followed by two musicians with squeaking fiddles and also by two men firing off continually a couple of old rusty fowling pieces, to the great admiration of the young folks.

After them came the figure, and the procession was closed by all the rest of the inhabitants. At every twenty or thirty steps they would all kneel down and pray audibly.

We smoothed our faces as we best could, not wishing to be supposed to know anything about the maize, just then.

On our return, we passed through a large town inhabited by the Pueblo Indians, called Tesuque. Here I first saw the singular custom which these Indians have of making the entrance to their houses by a ladder placed against the second-story window, there being no opening to the lower story.

This makes each house an easily-defended place, for the raising of the ladder leaves no easy ingress.

The village looked pretty, numerous bowers of green branches being erected outside the place to protect the women and children from the sun while making the earthen jars I have previously mentioned.

I learn there is a town inhabited by those Indians about six miles west of Taos, near the Rio Grande, called Taos Pueblo, the foundations of which occupy the whole of a half-acre of ground.

Commencing with a first story without windows, with merely a large hole into which they can drive, in danger, the greater part of their stock, and occupied as a storage room for the large quantities of corn which they improve their lonely improvements in cultivating (sic), the next story is got up to by another ladder, and so is continued the ladder until it reaches the top, which is seven-story high.

The second-story being drawn in a few feet smaller than the first, and so continued clear up to the top story, which is occupied by the Chief and on top of all is placed, in any entire danger of an army, a sentinel.

Also around the first story is strongly cemented with mud an adobe wall, two or three feet high, as a breast-work which, without no doubt, would keep, with but little resistance, away an army of 12 thousand Indians . . .

On my return to Fort Defiance, I found it mightily changed from its bad into good qualities, the quarters of the officers being rebuilt the third time: first with rough top, chinked and plastered with the abounding clay; 2nd with hewn logs; 3rd with stone; and a flag-staff also was erected upon which waved the elegant red, white, and blue of the United States. A fine corral was also now enumerated of the Quartermaster's cattle and sheep, also mules and horses, and a new Commanding Officer which, as soon as I returned, sent his Orderly for me, desiring to know of me what berth at the post I would deem best suitable for my ability. And let him know, and he would welcome me in the deepest of kind-ness, as my native ancestors were fond acquaintances of his, Capt. and Bvt. Major H. L. Kendrick, Command-ing officer of Battalion, and Commanding officer of Com-pany B, 2d Regiment of U. S. Artillery.

A Dramatic Theater was started by several members of the Battalion, and patronized by all the officers, in one of the rooms formerly occupied by a squadron of Dra-goons. Our men had converted it into a handsome theatre.

A good wardrobe and suitable scenery were procured with great difficulty, but in the middle of the month of May until I received my discharge, we opened with *Pizarro*, and *Bombastes Furioso*, and *The Scottish Shoe-maker and His Wife*. In which we soon opened to a crowded house.

Our greatest difficulty was on the score of female per-formers, being obliged to take them from the ranks; but, luckily, three of the society made very good-looking women when dressed in character.

About the first of May, an order No. 78 was received by the Commanding Officer from the Adjutant General Officer – R. {Roger} Jones, Headquarters War Depart-ment, Washington, for private J. M. Rice, B Co. 2d Arty., to be discharged. I was sent for and those words struck my thoughts like a bullet. "My friend, Rice, I have to dis-charge you, and I am very sorry to part with you. But I strongly expect to proceed to Sacramento, this fall, and if you take your discharge now you will not receive a cent of your pay or allowances, which amount to nigh $300, and if you wish to serve your time in full, which you have already one-half, I will write to the Command-ing Officer of the Department, and get your time – in-cluded, also, all your allowances.

You can have just as long as you wish, and remain in the duty you are in, to subside your mind."

Now I was to stand {i.e., decide} if proper to accept my discharge or not. At last, my thoughts run to that kind Father who had, in my desire, gone to a great trouble and expense for his only eldest son and it was my duty to repay him, if possible, which {i.e., so} I took the glowing Eagle of a discharge – called a Buzzard by all the soldiers – and returned on my homeward march.

ILLUSTRATIONS

Inscription, Rock,,
Navajo, Cuntrey,

Black, Rock.
One. and a half, Mile South of
Fort Defiance.

Natural Spurs on the Kenical Grande,
Navajo Country

Tributary of the Scenical Grande
Navajo, Cuntry,

A scene on "Rock Creek, Setting down Battery
Apache Contrey "U.C".

Scene on the Plain, & Apache Ind°.

"The Cassa Grande"

"Navajo Contry"
U.C.

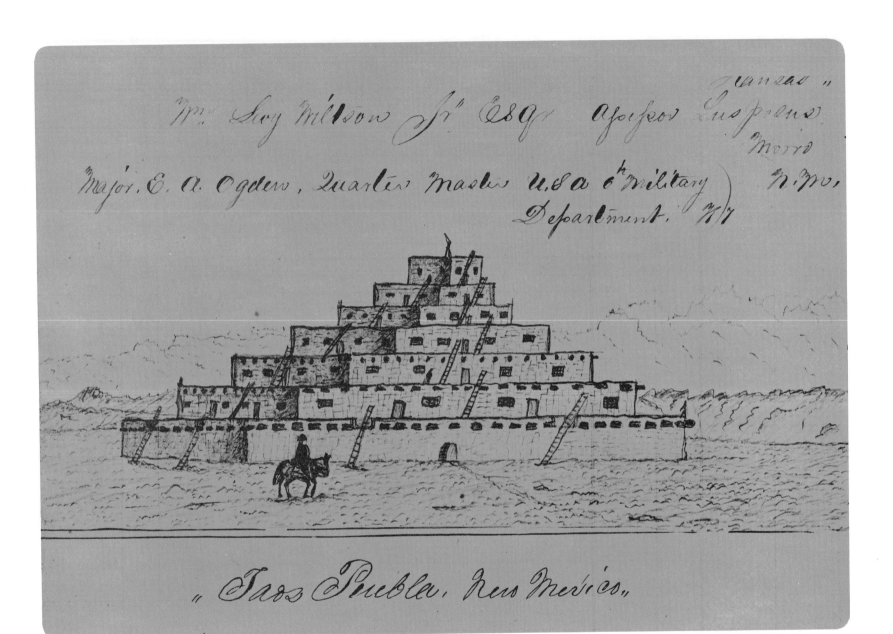

Wm. Secy Willson Jr. Esqr Apcheo Susperens
Morro
Major. E. A. Ogden, Quarter Master U.S.A 6th Military N.W.
Department.

"Taos Puebla. New Mexico,"

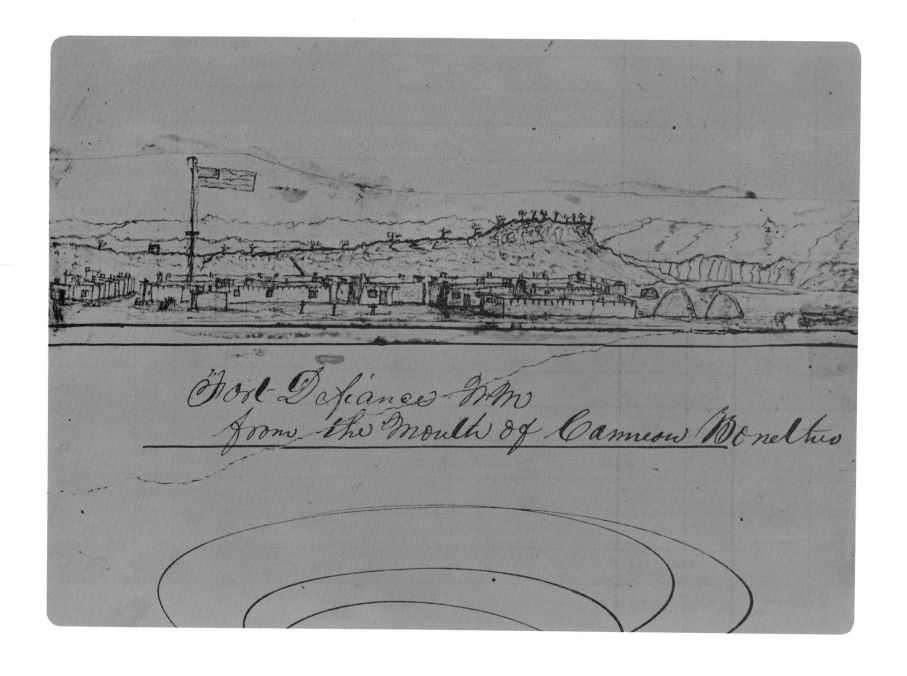

"Fort Defiance NM
from the mouth of Cannion Boneltio

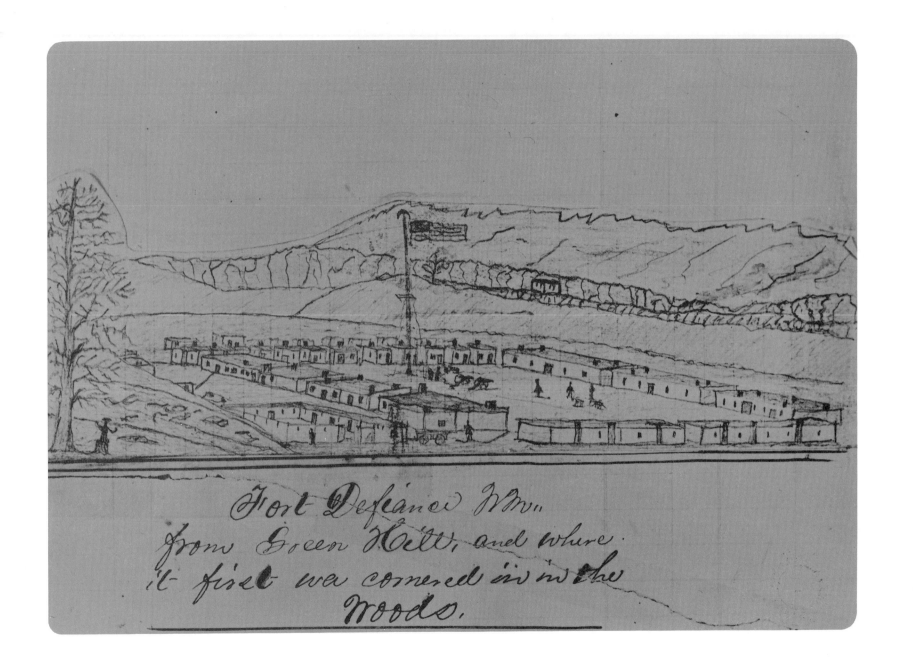

Fort Defiance N.M.
from Green Hill, and where
it first was cornered in in the
Woods.

The Extensive valley of Bonethis,
from "Booby Hill Fort Defiance N Mexico.

Cameron Bonettes.

from Do. extremities 1/3 Miles from S. Do.

Annen's Bonethe.

from upper extremities, or source T. D.

"Natural Melting House Rock,"
4 Miles South of Fort Defiance, N.M.

A View of Natural Bridge from Lower side
Few miles south of Fort Defiance N'M'

Hay Camp 7" Miles South of
Fort Defiance."

F. W. Rice Esq Campaign in Mn 180

Napoleon F. W. Rice F. W. Rice

Jackson J. M. Rice Napoleon

Michigan Elizabethtown Jackson

Essex County Mich

F. W. Rice N York

Wm W W Rice

F. W. Rice

Grazing Camp 5 Miles west of
Fort Defiance

Fort Defiance, New Mexico,
by
J. M. Rice,
Howitzer, Co. B. 2d Regmt U.S. Army

"Fort Leavenworth" Nebr Territory

Fort Union, New Mexico, in June,
1855

TABLE OF DISTANCES TRAVERSED

DATE	NAME OF ENCAMPMENTS	NO. OF MILES	TOTAL MILES	DATE	NAME OF ENCAMPMENTS	NO. OF MILES	TOTAL MILES
" 9	Diamond Spring to Cottonwood Fork	24	168	March 6th 1851			
" 10	In camp (rain)			" "	Plattsburgh to Whitehall	100	100
" 11	Cottonwood Fork to Turkey Creek	29	197	" 7	Whitehall to Albany; Cars	78	178
" 12	Turkey Creek to Little Arkansas River	25	222	" 8	Albany to New York; Boat	160	338
" 13	Little Arkansas to Cow Creek	23	245	April 7	New York to New Orleans; Boat	1800	2138
" 14	Cow Creek to Arkansas Bend	22	267	May 6	New Orleans to Jefferson Barracks	1200	3338
" 15	Arkansas Bend to Pawnee Fork	35	302	" 14	Jefferson Barracks to Fort Leavenworth	330	3668
" 16	In camp (on account of high water)				ON THE PLAINS OF INDIAN TERRITORY		
" 17	Pawnee Fork to Coon Creek	16	318	May 30	Fort Leavenworth to Eleven Mile Creek	11	11
" 18	Coon Creek to Arkansas River	25	343	June 1st	Eleven Mile Creek to Rock Creek	15	26
" 19	Along the Arkansas River	24	367	" 2	Rock Creek to Kansas River	10	36
" 20	" do " "	23	390	" 3	In camp (waiting for train)		
" 21	" do " "	23	426	" 4	Kansas River to Eleven mile (sic) Grove	20	56
" 22	Ditto, Crossings	23	446	" 5	Elm Grove to 110 Mile Creek	22	78
" 23	" do " "	20	468	" 6	Ditto, above, to Rock Creek	21	99
" 24	" do " "	22	490	" 7	Rock Creek to East of Big St. John's Spring	23	122
" 25	" do " "	19	509	" 8	Big St. John's Spring to Diamond Spg.	22	144

DATE	NAME OF ENCAMPMENTS	NO. OF MILES	TOTAL MILES
" 26	" do " "	22	509
" 27	Along the Arkansas River to Bent's Fort	20	529
" 28	" do " " " "	20	529
" 29	Do., to Mouth Purgatoire Creek	15	562
" 30	to Aug [July] 1st in camp 12 miles below Bent's Fort		
July 2nd	To Timpa Creek (west of Arkansas)	39	601
" 3	To another camp on same creek	7	608
" 4	To Hole in the Rock	23	631
" 5	To Purgatoire Fork	30	661
" 6	To foot of the Ratón Mountains	7	668
" 7	Within the Ratón Mountains	15	683
" 8	To Río Colorado (Canadian North Fork)	16	699
" 9	In camp (resting animals)		
" 10	To Río Bermejo	22	721
" 11	To Rayado (near Poñil)	20	741
" 12	To Ocaté	22	763
" 13	To Lower Mora Settlements	29	792
" 14	To Las Vegas	17	809
" 15	To first San Miguel Settlements (Tecolote)	18	827
" 16	To Susano	18	845
" 17	To Pecos (ruins and rancho)	17	862
" 18	Santa Fe	28	890
Measurement of Lieut. Emory of Topographical Engineers			883

SANTA FE TO FORT DEFIANCE

1851

DATE	NAME OF ENCAMPMENTS	NO. OF MILES	TOTAL MILES
Aug. 17th	Santa Fe to La Magada	35	35
" 18	To Bernalillo	15	50
" 19	To Ranchos de Albuquerque	19	69

DATE	NAME OF ENCAMPMENTS	NO. OF MILES	TOTAL MILES
" 20	In camp (grazing animals)		
" 21	" " do "		
" 22	" " do "		
" 23	Albuquerque to Río Puerco	20	89
" 24	Río Puerco to Sheep Springs	13	102
" 25	Sheep Springs to Laguna Creek	12	114
" 26	Laguna Creek to Cubero	12	126
" 27	Cubero to Ojo del Giah, Río	16	142
" 28	Ojo del Giah, Río to Cold Springs	27	169
" 29	"Frio Ojo," to Inscription Rock	16	185
" 30	Inscription Rock to Ojo del Pescado	16	201
" 31	Ojo del Pescado to Zuñi	12	213
Sept. 1st	Zuñi to Los Pozos	25	248
" 2	Los Pozos to Little Río Puerco	7	255
" 3	Little Puerco River to Willow Springs [Ojo del la Jarra?]	8	263
" 4	Willow Springs to Hay Camp	34	297
" 5	Hay Camp to Cañon [Cañoncito] Bonito or Fort Defiance	9	306

Measurement of Bvt. Maj. Kendrick, Capt. U.S.A. & Cmd. 2d Arty Cañon [Cañoncito] Bonito to Cañon de Chelly.

September 1851

DATE	NAME OF ENCAMPMENTS	NO. OF MILES	TOTAL MILES
" 7	Cañon [Cañoncito] Bonito along Valley Bonito	17	
" 8	Along Valley Bonito	39	56
" 9	Camp on Cienga Grande	31	88
" 10	Among Spurs on Cienga Grande	40	128
" 11	Camp on Rocks	50	178

DATE		NAME OF ENCAMPMENTS	NO. OF MILES	TOTAL MILES
"	12	Camped in Valley de Chelly	46	224
"	13	Into Cañon de Chelly	14	238
"	14	Marched out of Cañon de Chelly into Valley	14	252

Measurement of Lieut. Griffin, U.S. Army & Comp. B Com 2d Arty Cañon de Chelly to Río Gila.

September 16th 1851

DATE		NAME OF ENCAMPMENTS	NO. OF MILES	TOTAL MILES
"	"	Along Valley de Chelly	37	
"	17	" do. "	39	76
"	18	" do. "	35	111
"	19	"Frio Ojo" Springs	47	158
"	20	In camp (resting animals)		

Sept. 21st 1851

DATE		NAME OF ENCAMPMENTS	NO. OF MILES	TOTAL MILES
"	"	To Rock Creek	24	182
"	22	Along Rock Creek	44	226
"	23	To Head Waters of Río St. John (San Juan)	28	254
"	24	Along the Río St. John	32	286
"	25	Camp on a sandy plain	20	306
"	26	To headwaters of Río San Pedro [?]	39	345
"	27	Along Río San Pedro	34	379
"	28	" do. "	28	407
"	29	" do. "	27	434
"	30	" do. "	40	474
Oct.	1st	" do. "	50	524
"	2	Camp in Arroyo	29	553
"	3	Camp on Apache Plains	29	582
"	4	" " do. "	52	614
"	5	Struck the Rio Gila	39	653

DATE		NAME OF ENCAMPMENTS	NO. OF MILES	TOTAL MILES
"	6	Along Río Gila to Junction of San Pedro and Gila	100	753
"	7	Laid in camp refreshing animals until Oct. 12th		
"	13	Marched back	29	782
"	14	Marched and encamped on Gila	98	880
"	20	Strange camp in woods	24	907
"	21	Camp Thirst, without water	34	941
"	22	Camp on Night Creek	47	988
"	23	Camp on Badger Creek	44	1032
"	24	Struck and Encamped on Canon de Chelly	49	1081
"	25	Camp in Valley de Chelly	12	1120
"	26	Camp at mouth of Canon de Chelly	12	1120
"	27	In camp (resting animals)		
"	28	Camp in the woods	20	1140
"	29	Camp in Cañon [Cañoncito] Bonito	29	1169
"	30	Camp at Pan Okethe [?]	30	1199
"	31st	In Quarters in Fort Defiance	17	1216

Measurement of 1st Lieut. Griffin, U.S. Army & Com'dg Co B 2d A. Marched and Rode by Josiah M. Rice Hot'z Co. B 2d A.

DATE	MARCHED AT	MILES TOTAL
March 6th	Plattsburgh to Fort Leavenworth	3,668
May 15	Fort Leavenworth to Santa Fe	890
August 17	Santa Fe to Fort Defiance	306
Sept. 8	Fort Defiance to Cañon de Chelly	252
" 16	Cañon de Chelly to Río Gila and back to Fort Defiance	1,216
	Total	5,732

This is a short part of my journey when I am at home once more. But in my eye, it looks like a grave before me. But, Oh God, spare my life to reach that happy home in a civilized country once more, and I will chance to stay in my glory.

And I can tell you from experience, my young friends, if you desire to roam, take a land route, and your strong minds will soon get turned to your once-home fireside, with your father and kind mother to nourish you, if you are sick or in pain. Oh, when in sickness and no one to say, "Dear fellow, how do you feel this morning?" But if you give a sore groan, ready to give you a kick for doing so.

I am very respectfully
your obt. Servt.
Josiah M. Rice

A Private Soldier of
Howitzer Co. B, 2d
Regiment of U.S. Arty

As I am on my way to my friends I send this in advance, not thinking you will look for me too soon. Although, in time, I am in hopes you may not forget yourselves in blind eyes to pick out mistakes and bad writing, although I have improved my time in chopping whilst writing.

THE VALLEY OF THE DIAMONDS

Of Sinbad the Sailor of course you have read
But Sinbad has been for some centuries dead
And the vally of Diamonds no longer was known
Till the doctor found out we had one of our own
That the knowls are all covered with stones red, white,
    and green
With rubis and diamonds as brillient as ever was seen
Diamonds glowing like myrades of suns
And saphires igniting the charge in our guns
Let the tidings proclaim as the newspaper's say
That a soldier has nothing to do all the day
But crawl on his knees, ore New Mexico's hills
Whilst his pockets with jewels he constantly fills
You gapping greenhorns not landed a week
Who left the old country your fortunes to seek
Now is the moment your fortune's to make
If a trip to the Navajo Nation you take
Don't seek for employ, for wages are small
Nor say to yourself that you will wait until fall
No money is wanted, just take my advice
Enlist as a soldier, and youl be here in a trice
The Government kindly expences will bare
Youl have rations and pay and clothing to ware
A wagon to ride in all day lest to tire
And a detail at night to furnish you wood for fier
How glorious the prospects held forth to our view
Razed but not a moment what I tell you is true

Your rations are plenty, your pay is quite large
You are genteely supported at Government charge
At least with us at our neatly built fort
All other yarnes folks tell you are sport
How we must work in mud too our knees
And travel some miles, two chop down trees
How in tents we must lay, whilst our quarters must build
Thou hard work and starvation, half the Soldiers have
      killed
Our rations run out, and to find ourselves food
We are forced to hunt pinneons, a part of the day
      in the woods
How for coffyee we oft-times have had to substute wheat
Or for six weeks, or more we cant see any meat
How at first Indians sold pinneons cheap as dirt
And lately gave but a pint for a shirt
How our backs we must strip our poor bellys to fill
And staggering with hunger we are forced to work still
And mutter or grumble or speak a cross word
The sargent is ready with stock and with cord
And when bucked as a warning to all who are near
That we are expected their trouble to share
With Soldier like pacience, and Christian reliance
Until our Uncle feels pleaded to releave Fort Defiance
Heed not those yarnes my relative friends
Folks tell them to father their own private ends
They don't like that you our Diamonds should know
So invent all the stories of hunger and snow
You have the words of a Doctor, a Scholar, and a poet
And of course youl admit he ought to know it
He says the real Valley of Diamonds is here
So enlist and your fortunes are made, never fear

A Peace of Poetry Composed by the
Soldiers off Fort Defiance, N.M.
After the Starvations, in the fall of 1851
Josiah M. Rice Company B, 2nd Artillery

Letter from
   Courier Office, Conneautville, Crawford Co., Pa.
   October 19th 1852
"J.M. Rice, Dear Nephew:
   Your letter of July 25th reached me last night, I have written you several times in reply to your letters, as has also your mother, but it appears you do not get one letter.
   We are all well and prospering in business. Your mother suffers a great deal on your account. She is anxious to see you and hopes as soon as you are relieved from the Army you will come directly to her.
   You were a minor when you enlisted. And if your father was disposed to interest himself in your favor, he could forward your relief.
   If it is a possible thing to get released, do so. But, by no means, endeavor to escape without an honorable discharge.
   Let us hear from you often, and be assured that every letter you write shall be immediately answered, whether you receive it or not.

Should you receive this, write again and I will write you at greater length.

The stones you sent, some time ago, does not possess as much value as you supposed. Yet, keep them and bring them home as they possess some value.

Yours truly, friend and Uncle, G. W. Brown

Letter from
Conneautville, Pa.
Saturday October 21, 1852
My Dear Son

It is with unspeakable pain that I can seek to address you once more by pen after hearing the sad news of your fatal execution. O', my Boy, may it never be your unhappy fate, and may those that hold you dear as life, although the deep waters roll between us, never be the unhappy victim of such heart-rendering tidings.

October 14th we received a letter from Mary. She was well and said doing well. Her husband was in Vermont State to work, and they talked of moving there this fall.

She furthermore wrote that the news came to the Valley in a newspaper that one J. M. Rice was hung, but did not write me the particulars as she should of done.

And from that time, until the 19th of the same, I was nearly distracted, when, to my happy surprise, I found in our paper, sent from your Uncle's office, a letter from you, dated in New Mexico July 25th.

And may I now rejoice to hear it was no worse with you. Yes and you may do so, too. Oh, had I wings, now soon would your Mother fly and receive her once darling child, but, alas, Fate, has changed the . . . {blank, Ed.}. We are widely separated, and must try too reconcile ourselves to our best yet.

May the same Protector that has thus far protected, while many of your comrades has fallen, be with you, and guard and guide you to your native land again.

Oh, Josiah, be watchful, be faithful, and above all be prayerful and God will protect you, my lone boy. Do not give up to grief, but trust in Him that is able to redeem the soul. Although many can kill the{e} bodily, but God forbid they kill yours.

We all have wrote to you, and you did not write in you last letter that you had received one of them.

Your brother has sent two letters for your reprieve and what is more necessary to help you will be done by some of us, if made known.

I should think a petition ought to be granted. Will not the officers have sympathy for disconsolate parents, bereft of all that is near and dear on earth, when separated from their children?

Me thinks I hear them say, "Go, Boy, to thy Mother that holds the{e} the most dear, and be her comfort in declining years."

Should these lines prove true to their mission, may it be God's will and the will of man you shall be set at liberty again. And should it be granted, you will stand, many times, the exposure of sudden calamities and as one to administrate relief. You have a long road to travel to find your friends again. But, be prudent in all your ways and works, and may it be our happy lot to meet again on earth.

Our friends here are all well at this time. We wish you to keep writing. Do not delay; it takes nearly three months for your letters to reach us. Therefore, keep them going. I must draw to a close by wishing you a reprieve and a speedy return to your kindred land again. Please accept of all our best loves and wishes to guide you in your lone pride. Franklin, he was here but a day or two ago, and was well, he is a bowsman on the canal. He will leave soon and board here and go to school. This from your would-be happy mother by your safe return.

P. H. Graves
To J. M. Rice

My dear Mother,

In relation to your feelings towards me I must request of you not to borrow trouble or molest thyself none the least, for it is all in vain. That once child, which you so oft used to rely upon to soothe your deep compassion, when your heart was beating in strong anguish, has wandered astray. But cast your mind upon him in a shadow, and say, "Farewell, lad. You would not accept a mother's kind and hopeful compassion by a kind advice. But rambled away from your native land into a wild, deserted, country, among tremendous roaming bands of savages, which daily attempt your life."

Once and a while, when trying to pacify my reflecting mind by a lonely ramble down the projecting, over-hung with willow, banks of a small brook, which bends its curling waters past our beautiful solitude, my mind reflects to that once-happy home, where so oft in my sports, and companions' play, jumping and capering like the sporting lamb, in the Spring of the year, and my childhood schools, and companions.

Oh could I but once more improve that time again.

But, dear mother, sorrow not, or molest yourself not for me, for I will soon join with you in your compassions and desirous feelings. I must draw to a close by bidding you farewell. I have improved the leisure opportunities by keeping a small journal.

By a favorite blessing, I am in
hopes of your comfort
I am, very respectfully,
Your obedient Servant and Son

Josiah M. Rice
Howitzer Co. B 2nd Regiment
of US Artillery
Fort Defiance Navajo Country New Mexico

9th Military Department
Fort Defiance, N. M. March 9th/1853

My dear Uncle, Mother, and Brother:

In a long absence, when I meditate my roaming mind in my daily operations and soldier duties, and, at night, when on my post as a sentinel guarding my country and soldier companions from their instant fatal danger, (and the native wolf and treacherous Indian prowl around, my instant fate and careless being with their most dolesome and melancholy cries), my mind reflects back to that once-happy dominion in a far-distant land which I never expect to see again, where so oft I have sported away many a childhood day in sorrow.

But, alas, Fate and a roaming mind has led me astray.

But if it be the will of that well-known Being to spare our joyful healths and lingering lives, we will, either sooner or later, meet in joy again. But the aid of that well-known Being and Providence urges me to proceed further into the wild, savage, wilderness. Although it is only banishment that I consider myself in, the fathomless center of an unknown habitation to none but the wild savage of the unboundless wood, it is telling no falsehood to relate my feelings to say that I am no less than thirteen hundred miles from the white features of the civilized race, except the mingled race of Mexicans, who are entirely much treacherous, although half-savage themselves. It is truly dangerous to travel in, or through, this country in safety. In the first place, if you are improving your leisure opportunities by a lonely ramble in the wild forest, and the savage Indian attacks you, he will surely have your scalp, if not Your danged life.

Also, if you escape and seek a Mexican settlement or town for security or safety, and you are suspicioned to contain or have the price or value of a common suit of Clothes, a Mexican will surely have the prize of your life, in return, if you are not prepared for defence.

It is no criminal circumstance to see every Native, as well as American, carry, attached to a fancy belt around the waist in a leather (pointed with silver) scabbard; a large butcher knife and, frequently, a revolving pistol. And if you chance to unite in any urging dispute whatever, the revolver or knife is, at once, introduced for a settlement. And many and many is the unlucky fatal being that has found a comfortable and lonely grave, unknown to none (sic) but the meddlesome, bountiful, wolves, which is deposited in the numerous drifting sands which multiply this desert, rolling, country.

It is fatiguing in the eyes of my companions at home to relate my feelings, to say that you may travel, mile after mile, over this sandy, rolling, country without attracting your attention by seeing vegetation of any sort or kind, except along the banks of streams. Although, on the banks of streams, the general growth of timber insists of cottonwood, scrub oak, willow, with, now and then, an occasional bastard red cedar.

The natives, on account of the entire absence of rain in this country, are forced to dig a *acequia* or ravine, adjoining it to the upper parts of the stream, in order to water their land sufficient to allow them to cultivate the soil. In this way, they manage to cultivate Indian corn and Chelecolorow {*chili colorado*} in Spanish, or red pepper, in English, to furnish themselves with the exceptions of when they go without, although the natives of the Río {Grande} del Norte manage to cultivate onions, wheat, Indian corn, red pepper, watermelons, muskmelons, squashes, pumpkins, besides large quantities of fruit and grapes. But, as for potatoes, I haven't seen one since leaving Fort Leavenworth, Nebraska Territory, although I learn they grow wild in the southern parts of Mexico. And on account of their great industry in making their mud huts and raising large onions, and running water uphill, they are truly noted for the same.

The high lands generally produce a species of pine or piñon so called by the Natives which yields a small oval round nut and in size of an ordinary chestnut. On this Natives not infrequently are forced to substitute [i.e., subsist] without the aid or subsistence of any other substitute for months, and especially during the winter season when no other subsistence is to be conveniently had.

Also on the highlands is found a species of white pine and bastard cedar. From this tree the natives collect a sort of berry, which makes, when pressed in a mill, a very good drink. But as the pine has a resorted spot for itself, it is seldom found among other trees. On the plains is seldom found any timber or vegetation of any sort or kind, except now and then a species of prickly pear, or Spanish bayonet, or *Lattillus*. On this shrub is a long prick from eighteen to thirty inches in length and those projecting out in every direction, and out of the center of all grows a stalk yielding from four to twelve pears which, when green and if roasted, serve the appetite the place of bread and meat and, when ripe, are a light orange color and taste very much like a pineapple. On this fruit

it is known an Indian will travel mile after mile without the assistance of any other substitute (sic).

Also is found another cactus which grows no less than twelve to eighteen inches in height and from six to ten inches in diameter, while around its body is found a rib projecting out two or three inches more than its body. On suspicion of, and to protect itself from, its treacherous, waylaying enemy, is numerous thorns.

And if you are traveling over or through this wide defiled country and nearly famished with thirst for the want of that element which moistens your parching body, and gives glorifying strength to your weary legs which is seldom found on those wide sandy desert rolling plains and you become the eye-witness to one of these herbs, it is a happy relief to your unknown thirst, on approaching it and cutting it open and finding sufficient liquid or juice to refresh you.

In fact, this country is of an unbounded shape, being the mingled race of Mexicans and those tribes which settled by none but the wild savages themselves, except formerly resided in the United States and which, by the settling of the white people, have been driven back, mile after mile, until they are forced to contrast with this drouthful sandy country.

But as they cannot rely or furnish themselves with food by their well-known occupation of planting and hunting, they go down on the Río [Grande] del Norte among the bastard race, and supply themselves with large herds of cattle, sheep, goats, maize, and, if wanting any slaves, take away the inhabitants. On account of these cruel perennial depridations, the United States are forced to keep a standing army to prevent them. But, for instance, a company of the bold U.S.A. is stationed at Los Alamos and if the Indians feel disposed to drive away a flock of sheep in the vicinity of the town, they will delay, deposited behind the numerous sand banks, until the gloomy night stills the inhabitants of the town in deep repose then slowly, calmly, and still, the Indians will descend to where they see the herd at the close of day deposited, and kill the herder if any, and chase away the flock in the direction of whence they came. In the morning you will hear of the sad facts, and receive orders to saddle up your nag and follow in pursuit of them. But by the time you have prepared and followed in pursuit of them over the rolling sands with your American steed five or six miles, he is completely – on account of his numerous fatigues and starvations for the want of food – given out, and you are forced to turn back without the uncaptured foe.

I am happy to inform you that I received an application from you the 1st of January 1853, and also from my dear mother, and was happy to refer back to you and her again. But in relation to your applications beforementioned by you and Mother, I haven't received them. I received one from you dated May 6th/52, also another October 19th/52, also at the same time I received one from Mother, and this the only one, dated October 24th/52.

As I related in my other letter, Maj. Kendrick expected to go to San Diego, Upper California. I now must inform you that he has subsided (sic) to delay until fall, when he is sure to proceed, although his expedition to the Río Gila is expedient as our limbers of the Battery are packed in readiness. Also Capt. [John] Pope and Lieut. [William] Emory, two well-tried Engineer Officers are on their way to this post, and orders in the Act'g Asst. Post Adjutant's Office for Maj. H. L. Kendrick to proceed with the two Engineer Officers and his company as an escort without delay to the Cañon de Chelly and, after a successive explore from head to foot, to proceed with his escort and the two Engineer Officers to the Río Gila and there ascertain a favorite spot to establish a post and when his orders is approved of, return back to Fort Defiance and report to Col. Sumner. As I informed you, my Father was trying to get me my discharge. I have not received it yet but remain in hopes. I am well and enjoying the best of gloomy confessions and hope the few lines may find you partaking of the same blessings. Apply as soon as you get this, and I will apply also in return. Please place this before all encouraging friends. I must draw to a close by saying, alas, farewell. I will meet you again.

I am very respectfully, Your ob't Servt and Nephew

Josiah M. Rice

Howitzer Co. B 2d Arty, Fort Defiance, N.M.

INDEX

*A CANNONEER
IN NAVAJO COUNTRY*
was designed by
Paul Weaver,
set in the Aldus type of Herman Zapf,
and printed at Northland Press
on Beckett Laid Text
in an edition of 1500 copies.